Wittgen.

BFI Publishing

Wittgenstein

THE TERRY EAGLETON SCRIPT
THE DEREK JARMAN FILM

First published in 1993 by the
British Film Institute
21 Stephen Street
London W1P 1PL

Reprinted 1993

British Library Cataloguing-in-Publication Data.
A Catalogue record for this 1993 book
is available from the British Library.

ISBN 0 85170 396 8
      0 85170 397 6 pbk

Design by Cinamon Designs.

Printed in Great Britain by
The Trinity Press, Worcester

BANDUNG – 'THE PHILOSOPHERS' Three years ago, the Commissioning Editor, Education, at Channel 4 asked me to develop an idea for a series on Philosophy. After some thought, I suggested a set of one-hour dramas based on the lives, times and ideas of a set of philosophers from Ancient Greece to modern times. The original plan was to do a total of twelve over three years. Four scripts were commissioned – *Socrates* by Howard Brenton, *Spinoza* by Tariq Ali, *Locke* by David Edgar, *Wittgenstein* by Terry Eagleton.

Department budget cuts meant that we could only do three. *Spinoza – the Apostle of Reason,* was directed by Chris Spencer and is already in the can. *Wittgenstein* grew and grew till it became a Derek Jarman film. Locke will be directed by Peter Wollen and is due for filming in May/June 1993.

TARIQ ALI

A complete catalogue
of Bandung documentaries/dramas is available from:

Bandung Ltd
Block H
Carkers Lane
53–79 Highgate Road
London NW5 1TL

PREFACE

Colin MacCabe

There can be very few films which see no change between
the original script and the final screen version. First there
are what one might describe as the technical difficulties.
The budget will not allow thousands of extras or the build-
ing of a particular set. As vital, the sun may refuse to shine
for an exterior which must be bathed in light and the whole
scene has to be dropped. But, over and above such external
pressures, is the perpetual process of collaboration which
makes film such a clearly different form to written fiction.

One can argue, Derek Jarman probably would argue, that
every single member of the cast and crew actively partici-
pates in the creative decisions of the film. He writes, in his
introduction, that his philosophy of film is to 'Have no plan.
Then you can allow your collaborators to take over.' Few
directors embrace such ultra democratic views, but even the
most authoritarian must, however, engage his actors in a
collective effort to bring the film into being. And as lines
gain intonation and pace, they inevitably change. More
radical, however, is the moment when the film enters the
cutting room and film suddenly appears as a visual reality
rather than a verbal sequence. At this point the film is effec-
tively written over again, but now using all the resources of
light and movement as well as speech.

There is then, I think, a real interest in reading and comparing the various verbal stages of any film. And this general interest becomes intense when we turn to *Wittgenstein*. There is the paradox of the subject matter: the attempt to represent the life of a thinker who fundamentally questioned our assumptions about representation. More, there is the striking juxtaposition between writer and director. Terry Eagleton, the most significant Marxist literary critic of his generation and Derek Jarman, the most consistently original film-maker of the last two decades.

It must be said that the transformations Jarman and Ken Butler brought to the original Eagleton screenplay are well in excess of the inevitable changes that attend any metamorphosis from script to screen. If budget may have been a factor in the abandonment of the Cambridge exteriors, the decision to provide a linear biographical frame is obviously a complete re-direction of the film. The exact significance of the changes is for the reader to judge. Eagleton sees the substitution of a figure of English eccentricity for his European philosophical modernist. Jarman stresses the focus on a black background against which the colours and Mr Green blaze – illuminating a queer life.

What is certain is that the final film is unthinkable without the original screenplay and that it draws much of its strength from it. At the same time there is no doubt that the film manages to go further than the screenplay – to articulate more of the extraordinary elements of Wittgenstein's life. As someone who spent a large part of his student life studying Wittgenstein in Cambridge, I was astonished at its accuracy about both place and topic. This accuracy, it must be stressed, is not a question of historical truth. When Keynes asks Wittgenstein, post-*Tractatus*, whether he is worrying about logic or his sins, the question is in fact taken from a pre-*Tractatus* discussion with Bertrand Russell. The V-sign that so startles Wittgenstein in the street was in fact a Neapolitan gesture with which the Italian economist Sraffa argued against a representational theory of language.

But these facts are easily consulted in Ray Monk's exemplary biography (Jonathan Cape: 1990). What the film does do is to juxtapose the social world of Cambridge – brilliantly caught in the performances of Keynes and Russell – with the very different and much more private world of Vienna. And it manages also, I think, to articulate in filmic form the great themes of Wittgenstein's thought: that language is not a representation of the world but part of it and that our most private experiences take shape in public form.

Finally, I think it captures the paradox of Wittgenstein's life which combined intense doubt and suffering with a joy in both life and thought, enabling his last words to be: 'Tell them I had a happy life.' It is not the least of the achievements of Jarman's film that it makes that final utterance more comprehensible.

INTRODUCTION TO WITTGENSTEIN

Terry Eagleton

The library of artistic works on Ludwig Wittgenstein continues to accumulate. What is it about this man, whose philosophy can be taxing and technical enough, which so fascinates the *artistic* imagination? Frege is a philosopher's philosopher, Bertrand Russell every shopkeeper's image of the sage, and Sartre the media's idea of an intellectual; but Wittgenstein is the philosopher of poets and composers, playwrights and novelists, and snatches of his mighty *Tractatus* have even been set to music. He was a myth in his own time, a kind of fictional character deposited in a depressingly real Cambridge; and there is a fabular or fairytale quality about his riches-to-rags career – the plutocrat father, the solitary hut by the Norwegian fjord, the doomed forays into school teaching, Galway, Stalinist Russia – which lends itself easily to literary or dramatic representation.

But it is more than a matter of the self-lacerating, spiritually anguished life. The *Tractatus*, one might claim, is the first great work of philosophical modernism – not a theoretical reflection on that avant-garde cultural experiment, but an example of it in its own right, the point where the modernist impulse migrates out of film and poetry and sculpture and comes to occupy philosophy itself from the inside. Its true coordinates are not Frege or Russell or logical positivism but Joyce, Schoenberg, Picasso. Like many a modernist work of art, the *Tractatus* secretes a self-destruct device within itself: he who understands these propositions, Wittgenstein remarks abruptly at its conclusion, will recognise that they are nonsense. For the *Tractatus*, absurdly, strives to articulate what it itself has placed under the censorship of silence – the relation of language to the world. And if what it says of that ineffable relationship is true, then it has itself no title to exist. The structure of language can manifest the way the world is, but it cannot speak directly of how it does this, for this would mean language getting a handle on itself, commenting in the act of showing us the world on the fit or distance between that world and itself. And this would be like trying to measure something with a ruler while trying in that very act to measure, with the same ruler, the distance between the object and itself. Only if we use these impossible propositions like ladders, kicked away as soon as mounted, will we see the world aright; and in this sense the *Tractatus* cancels itself out in a gesture of modernist irony, illuminates the truth only in the dim glare created by its sudden self-implosion. It is no accident that its author was a military volunteer who left for the trenches in the hope that the nearness of death might cast some light on his radically unfulfilling life.

It is not hard to find parallels to this ironic self-undercutting in modernist art as a whole, which can speak of a progressively degraded reality only out of the side of its mouth as it broods incessantly on its own crystalline forms. Something of the totalising hunger of modernism inspires this extraordinary treatise – to hold the world in a single thought! – but this at best is a Pyrrhic victory. For what this thought will deliver you is just the grim truth that the world has no truck with value. Value cannot be *in* the world, since it resides in the human subject; and the human subject is not an object within reality, but the limit or horizon which brings that reality into focus. This world which is baldly whatever is the case, whose value and meaning is always elusively elsewhere, is familiar enough to us from the great experimental art of the early twentieth century; and so too is that intense subjective inwardness which has now been banished to the edges of the universe, as rootless and exilic as a Wittgenstein in the Fens. There is an immense amount we can say, but none of it is particularly important; and this is not some banal existential inarticulacy of the 'if only I had words' variety, but an utterly rigorous demonstration in the most precise of linguistic terms of the limits inherent to discourse. The 'mystical' which lies beyond expression is not some spiritual trip, but absolutely nothing whatsoever, the very heart of negation.

If modernism is the point where painting comes to be about paint, sculpture about stone and literature about words, then the *Tractatus* is the place where philosophy begins to bend back on itself and interrogate its own medium, which is of course language itself. Instead of starting from the world and then seeing how language fits into it, modernist philosophy turns that relation on its head: 'the world' just is whatever our language discloses to us. The later Wittgenstein will pursue his lifelong preoccupation with language, that most prominent of all twentieth-century intellectual protagonists; but he will abandon the crystalline purity of his ascetic youth and seek to return us to the rough ground of our mixed, ambiguous, commonplace speech. Nothing could provide a greater contrast with the open-ended, pluralistic, generously demotic investigations of this later period than the man himself; imperious, dogmatic, haughtily patrician, driven by a fatiguing zeal for moral perfection and well-practised in brusquely casting off any involvement which seemed to stand in its way. The last thing Wittgenstein was was a Wittgensteinian, with the philosophic resonances that term now holds for us. He was an arresting combination of monk, mystic and mechanic: a high European intellectual who yearned for Tolstoyan *simplicitas*, a philosophical giant with scant respect for philosophy, an irascible autocrat with a thirst for holiness. But the puritanical severity of the *Tractatus*, where man and work were peculiarly at one, will now be syphoned out of the philosophy, which becomes a mere therapy for those languishing in the grip of linguistic delusions, and nurtured instead in an inner life so unremittingly intense that the slightest gesture or encounter could become the scene of some cosmic spiritual drama. Wittgenstein suffered all his life from that curious mania known as Protestantism, in which nothing is random or contingent, everything a potential sign of salvation or damnation; yet his later thought turns its back resolutely on such absolutism, on the pure ice of the beautiful inhuman metaphysics of the early vision, and embraces a world in which the only foundation – a slippery, variable one, sure enough – is our common institutional practices, as spontaneous and self-evident as a handshake. If this makes him in one sense an odd sort of materialist, it also provides an opening for a conservative reading of his works, much in favour in the pragmatist climate of our times. Philosophy renounces its hubristic vision of totality and embraces instead the mind-bending truth that everything happens exactly as it does; everything is exactly in its place, and philosophy can in no sense interfere with it. It is, in short, something of a mug's game, though in this case it takes an Emperor to realise that the Emperor is naked. Wittgenstein believed that he had solved all philosophical problems by solving that most vexed of problems, philosophy itself. But the man and the work are once more strangely at odds: for if the *Philosophical Investigations* would persuade us to accept our forms of life as simply given, the Wittgenstein who ran off to the Soviet Union to work as a doctor there was hardly enamoured of that form of life known as English society, and had some notably harsh things to say about its rulers.

If the early work holds one kind of attraction for the artist, the later writings manifest another. For they belong to that heretical subcurrent of philosophy which works by joke, anecdote, aphorism, by the striking image or gnomic saying, distilling a whole complex argument in some earthy dictum or sudden epiphany.   One thinks of the various jokers in the philosophical pack, from Kierkegaard and Nietzsche to Adorno and Derrida, those thinkers who could only say what they meant by inventing a whole new form of writing.   The *Tractatus* may have the shimmering purity of an Imagist poem or Suprematist canvas; but the *Investigations* read more like an assemblage of ironic fables or fragments of a novel, deceptively lucid in their language but teasingly enigmatic in their thought.   It is a thoroughly dialogical work, in which the author wonders out loud, imagines an interlocutor, asks us questions which may or may not be on the level.   Like the Freudian analyst, we suspect that he has some answers but is keeping them up his sleeve, forcing the reader into the work of self-demystification, genially engaging our participation by his deliberately undaunting style but running the odd ring around us into the bargain.   The truth lies there under our nose, so the work seems to intimate – but we could never of course grasp anything as scandalously self-evident as that, and prefer to peer at it instead through our imposingly metaphysical spectacles.   It is a seductive thought, analogous to Bertolt Brecht's notion of *plumpes Denken* or crude thinking, that if only we could empty the ideological garbage out of our heads, reinvent the wise naivety of our childhood, we would dissolve away our dilemmas and see the world aright; but this noble doctrine, as Henry Fielding remarked of the view that the virtuous will receive their reward in this world, has only one drawback, namely that it is not true.   Like all good artists, Wittgenstein is selling us less a set of doctrines than a style of seeing; and that style cannot be abstracted from the feints and ruses of his language, the rhetorical questioning and homely exemplifying, the sense of a mind in ceaseless ironic dialogue with itself.   Can there be a private language? Well, imagine someone who passes money from one of his hands to another and thinks he has made a financial transaction. Can criteria ever be other than public? Think of someone who cries 'But I know how tall I am!' and places his hand on top of his head. Does the simple repetition of an event confirm it? That would be rather like a man buying himself a second copy of the morning newspaper to confirm that what the first copy said was true. Here is the authentic Wittgensteinian style, wry, idiosyncratic, subduedly humorous – the idiom of a man effortlessly at home in a common world, which was the very last thing he was.

No one has more vehemently defended the notion of a private language than the Romantic artist, marooned with his transcendental wisdom in a blankly uncomprehending society. And it is here that Wittgenstein, for all his formidable Viennese cultivation, is most bracingly unromantic, in his relentless deconstruction of this consolatory myth. What the *Investigations* try to therapise us out of is just that Western bourgeois notion of 'inwardness' – of an inner life so deep, subtle and evanescent that it eludes the reach-me-down categories of our social existence. It is exactly this that some have found so unacceptable about his later thought, which on a crude interpretation is just a species of souped-up behaviourism, allergic to talk of 'mental processes' and 'inner experience'. This really *is* to travesty the work of a man who knew, if anyone did, all about 'inner experience'; but it is a symptom of the political prejudice of a rampantly individualist society that the later Wittgenstein's emphasis on the public nature of our most apparently private terms should have been resisted in this way. He lived a secret sexual life, but insisted that nothing was hidden; he appealed to the constitutive role of convention in all that we say and do, and had all the insouciant disdain for convention of the aristocrat. There is a split, here as elsewhere, between the man and the work, which the

Freudianism he thought no more than a tolerably interesting fiction might do well to examine. Long before contemporary cultural theory, Wittgenstein was teaching us that the self is a social construct – that when I look into my most secret feelings, I identify what I do only because I have at my disposal a language which belonged to my society before it ever belonged to me. There are some radical political implications in this way of seeing, though here, once again, the man and the philosophy are intriguingly disjunct. Politically speaking, Wittgenstein was for the most part a reactionary remnant of the Austro-Hungarian Empire, and if he was attracted to the Soviet Union it was for all the wrong reasons. Some of his best friends, as the old cliché has it, were on the Left; but there is little evidence he shared much in common with them, other than scorning the English middle classes from his own patrician end of the political spectrum as they condemned them from the other. Wittgenstein was historically displaced, out of his epoch, a man who profoundly wished that modernity had never happened and simply wanted it to go away; and in this sense too, oddly enough, he resembles the great artistic modernists, who were often at once archaic and avant-garde, buoyantly confronting an inconceivably transfigured future while fixing their gaze elegiacally on an unrecapturable past.

The brief I was given in writing a television play about Wittgenstein was to assume a more or less totally ignorant audience and dramatise something of his ideas in terms of his life. This, on any estimate, is a tallish order, partly because the life and the ideas happened, so to speak, consecutively. The most dramatically interesting events of Wittgenstein's life – Vienna, the political turmoil of central Europe, the first world war – took place before he became a philosopher, even if they left their indelible mark on what philosophy he produced. Derek Jarman's script tackles this problem by a kind of biographical montage, tracing a linear progress from childhood to Cambridge; I decided to place him at some historically indeterminate point in Cambridge and have him occasionally glance backwards. My own form is realist, Jarman's a good deal more adventurous and experimental. Both works weave quotations from Wittgenstein into imaginary material, and both try to convey something of the flavour of the man while communicating the main lines of his thought. The composite television text which results from the dovetailing of the two then interestingly dramatises the conflicts and disjunctions I have discussed above. Watching the finished film, it is hard for me at least to see how *this* man could have generated *these* ideas, which seem in certain key ways intriguingly out of character. My own script strikes me as reasonably strong on ideas but short on dramatic action; Jarman's, minus my own interpolations, seems to me just the other way round. It is, as it were, a very *English* text, for the English love 'a character' but are notably nervous of the intellect. Wittgenstein himself, according to F. R. Leavis, divided people into 'moral' and 'intellectual' types, and something of this fissure runs through the finished product. Wittgenstein was a deeply moral man – too moral by far, as Keynes argues in the play – but he committed the serious error of dissociating morality from the intellect, which is part of the way he became an honorary Englishman.

My own technique for bridging this gap was largely linguistic: to introduce into the 'real-life' scenes something of the verbal tautness, wit and pointedness of Wittgenstein's philosophical style. Jarman's script bathes in a very different emotional ethos – fanciful, whimsical, 'English' in this sense too – though what it loses, in my view, in sensibility, exchanging sharp for broad humour, it gains immensely in visual and dramatic interest. In any case, my point is that the disjunction between the two versions becomes itself a statement about the contradictions of the man; for Wittgenstein's writing is often extremely 'English' in tone, deliberately askew to the rationalist systematising of European thought, and at the same time deeply enigmatic and intractable. It was a body of work which lent itself, stylistically speaking, to a whole school of Oxbridge High Table philosophising, where the point seemed to be to pass the port and deny that there were any real problems at all, other than making sure the decanter wasn't empty when it came round for a second time. It was this trivialising style which led one of its most celebrated exponents to claim that he had talked an undergraduate student out of suicide by demonstrating to him that the grammar of 'nothing matters' differed logically from that of 'nothing chatters'. If Wittgenstein's style *could* license such inanities, then that makes a significant point about it; but at the same time it passes over what one might term the Germanic profundity of his intellect, the unrelenting passion and rigour beneath the laid-back homeliness.

In a curious sense, then, the composite script is true to Wittgenstein in its very structural dislocations, its clash of styles and emotional tones. For it is naive to imagine that there is some direct expressive relation between a life and the work it produces. That work may be related to the life as much by repression, sublimation, disavowal as by simple reflection, though Wittgenstein himself would have snorted at such psychoanalytic jargon. But though he would probably have dismissed such language out of hand in his honorary-English way, he was nevertheless a suitable case for treatment, and this is yet another of his multiple contradictions. 'It takes one Viennese to know another', he remarks scornfully of Freud in this play; and the ambivalence of that, identifying and rejecting simultaneously, says much about the clash of cultures, histories, sensibilities and styles of thought of which he remains such an endlessly fascinating example.

Ludwig Wittgenstein

THE TERRY EAGLETON SCRIPT

Characters

LUDWIG WITTGENSTEIN
BERTRAND RUSSELL
JOHN MAYNARD KEYNES
G. E. MOORE
DAVID JARRETT
FRANK MELLING
DAISY
MRS MOORE
MECHANIC
BUTLER
MONKS, MEMBERS OF SEMINAR, FELLOWS OF TRINITY,
THREE UNDERGRADUATES

Notes on Characters

WITTGENSTEIN – mid-forties, about 5' 6" tall, lean, handsome, blue eyes, wavy brown hair. Dressed throughout in an old sports jacket, open-necked shirt and patched baggy trousers. His accent is a curious mixture of German and upper-class English. Haughty, forceful, intense, austere.

RUSSELL – mid-forties; short and lean of build, with acquiline features and a shock of dark hair. A touch of the raffish aristocrat as well as of the high intellectual.

MOORE – about 50 years old, portly, pipe-smoking, ruddy complexion, with the lightest touch of Irish in his voice.

JARRETT – about 23 years of age, willowy, handsome, fair-haired, slightly cherubic features.

KEYNES – mid-forties, handsome, faintly languid, a touch of the aesthete about his dress and manner.

The play is set in the mid-1930s.

INT   CHAPEL   DAY

We are inside the chapel of a monastery in Austria. The monks are in their choir stalls, singing a Latin office in plain chant.

EXT   MONASTERY GARDEN   DAY

The garden of the monastery; sounds of plain chant still drift to our ears. A few monks in their habits are strolling in the garden walks. FRANK MELLING, *a Cambridge don in his late twenties, is wandering through the garden dressed in light white suit and boater hat, evidently in search of something. He comes up behind two young monks chatting to each other in German; they become aware of his presence and make way for him with a courteous smile.*

MELLING *halts suddenly, having sighted his goal. At the far end of the garden, a small bowed figure is hoeing a flowerbed.* MELLING *moves closer, slightly hesitant. The small man is dressed very simply, in open-necked shirt and patched baggy trousers.* MELLING *halts behind him.*

MELLING   Dr Wittgenstein.

WITTGENSTEIN *turns slowly towards him.*

Dr Wittgenstein, I have come to take you home.

WITTGENSTEIN

> *Eyeing him carefully; a long pause.*

Home? Where is that?

MELLING   Cambridge.

> WITTGENSTEIN *snorts incredulously and turns back to his hoeing.* MELLING *takes an envelope from his pocket.*

I have a letter from Mr Keynes for you.

> *Holds out envelope;* WITTGENSTEIN *ignores him, continues working.*

I'm sorry, I ought to introduce myself: Frank Melling.

WITTGENSTEIN   You are a philosopher?

MELLING   Yes; I'm a Fellow of Queens'.

WITTGENSTEIN   Then give it up; do something useful. Become a doctor.

MELLING

> *Fishing in his pocket again.*

I also have a letter from Mr Russell. He asked me to remind you ... (Hesitates).

WITTGENSTEIN   Well?

MELLING   He asked me to remind you, Dr Wittgenstein, that you are the greatest philosopher of our time.

WITTGENSTEIN   And you came all this way to tell me that?

MELLING   You're wasting your time here, sir – if I may say so.

WITTGENSTEIN   I'm saving my soul. Do you call that a waste of time?

MELLING   We need you in Cambridge, sir.

WITTGENSTEIN

Indicating flowerbed.

You see this flowerbed?

Thrusts his hoe into it.

It's just soil all the way down. You can't feel rockbottom. I thought I'd touched rockbottom.

MELLING   I beg your pardon?

WITTGENSTEIN   Logic. I thought I'd unearthed the fundamental structure of all language. But it's only a metaphor – just like the rest of philosophy.

MELLING   You really can't keep running away.

WITTGENSTEIN   Give up philosophy, Mr Melling. Get out while you still have a bit of a brain left. Be a mechanic. You see these flowers?

Indicates with a wave of his arm.

I planted them all; I tend them every day. What's philosophy to that?

MELLING   Cambridge needs you, sir.

WITTGENSTEIN

With sudden vehemence.

Cambridge is a cesspit.

MELLING   Your friends need you. If you won't come back for philosophy, come back for them.

Close up of WITTGENSTEIN's *face. He stares intently, almost fiercely at* MELLING, *then away, gazing up the garden, then back to* MELLING *again.*

EXT   TRINITY COLLEGE   LATE AFTERNOON

*The Great Court of Trinity College; a bell is toll-
ing five o'clock. General stir and hubbub: twenty
or thirty academics, young and middle-aged dons
and a sprinkling of students, are bustling across
the court in academic gowns, carrying books and
notepads. Two or three women among them.
They are heading for the foot of one of the stair-
cases.*

INT   BEDROOM   LATE AFTERNOON

WITTGENSTEIN *is sitting in semi-darkness on the
edge of his bed, in a bedroom which gives directly
onto his living room. His head is buried in his
hands; some slight writhing and groaning. Raises
his head: a face full of misery.*

WITTGENSTEIN   Intolerable, intolerable.

EXT   TRINITY COLLEGE   LATE AFTERNOON

The academics are milling around the foot of
WITTGENSTEIN*'s staircase, chatting as they as-
cend. We catch glimpses of* RUSSELL, MOORE *and*
KEYNES.

INT   STAIRCASE   LATE AFTERNOON

People are climbing the staircase to the door of
WITTGENSTEIN*'s room, which has 'MR WITT-
GENSTEIN' inscribed above it. There is a pile of
deckchairs outside the door; each person picks up
a deckchair and disappears with it into the room.*

INT   BEDROOM   LATE AFTERNOON

WITTGENSTEIN *is still sitting on the edge of the bed, head in hands, rocking slightly, moaning softly.*

INT   WITTGENSTEIN'S ROOM   LATE AFTERNOON

People are setting up their deckchairs and settling into them, chatting noisily. The room is almost bare of furniture: one armchair, a table and chair, a single empty deckchair already positioned at the front of the room, for WITTGENSTEIN *himself.*

INT   BEDROOM   LATE AFTERNOON

Light falls suddenly across WITTGENSTEIN's *face, as* DAVID JARRETT, *dressed in academic gown, opens the door cautiously and peers round.*

JARRETT   (Low voice) Ludwig, what are you *doing* in there?

WITTGENSTEIN

Without looking up.

Go away.

JARRETT   (Hissing urgently) Don't be so stupid. Russell and Moore are out there – you mustn't keep them waiting.

WITTGENSTEIN   Tell them to go away. I'm cleaned out; there's nothing in my head.

JARRETT

Coming into the bedroom.

Ludwig, you've got to come out this instant. No seminar, no flick, alright?

WITTGENSTEIN

> *Raising his head.*

What?

JARRETT   If you don't come out now I'm not going to the flicks with you.

WITTGENSTEIN

> *Head back in hands.*

Intolerable, intolerable.

JARRETT

> *Placing hand on* WITTGENSTEIN's *shoulder.*

Oh for God's sake, Ludwig, pull yourself together; you're not facing execution.

> *Crouches down beside him.*

Come on, old chap, up we come.

> *Puts hand under his elbow.*

That's the way. A flick for a seminar, OK?

> WITTGENSTEIN *totters grudgingly to his feet.*

Don't worry, you'll be fine; just open your mouth and say the first thing that comes into your head.

WITTGENSTEIN

> *Mutters crossly.*

Don't be so ridiculous.

> JARRETT *brushes down his jacket a little and smooths his hair.*

You're torturing me, David.

INT   WITTGENSTEIN'S ROOM   LATE AFTERNOON

> JARRETT *steers* WITTGENSTEIN *through the door of the bedroom to confront his audience, and slips unobtrusively aside. Excited murmurs of anticipation as* WITTGENSTEIN *shambles dazedly to his deckchair and sinks glumly into it. More rustling and murmuring from the academics, who then fall gradually silent, like a theatre audience waiting for curtain up.*

> WITTGENSTEIN *throws back his head with sudden violence and stares for a long time at the ceiling, an agonised expression on his face. He shakes his head vehemently, sinks it in his hands; then looks back up to the ceiling.*

> *We see* RUSSELL *and* MOORE *sitting together on the front row.*

MOORE

> *Low voice to* RUSSELL.

What's up with the fellow?

RUSSELL   Dunno. Touch of constipation, perhaps?

WITTGENSTEIN

> *With disturbing abruptness.*

A dog cannot lie. (Long pause) But neither can he be sincere.

> *Rustle of faint amusement from audience.*

A dog may be expecting his master to come. Why can't he be expecting him to come next Wednesday? Is it because he doesn't have language?

> *Eyes to ceiling once more; agonised expression; pause.*

If a lion could speak ... we would not be able to understand what he said. (Pause) Why do I say this? Moore, why do I say such a thing?

MOORE   I haven't the foggiest, Wittgenstein. If we can understand you I shouldn't think we'd have much trouble with a lion.

> *A few laughs, low exclamations, as the audience scent battle being joined.*

VOICE FROM BACK   We could always get an interpreter.

WITTGENSTEIN   Do you mean for me or for the lion?

> *General chuckles.*

Yes, we could get an interpreter. But of what possible use would that be?

> *Pause;* WITTGENSTEIN *looks round fiercely.*

To imagine a language is to imagine a form of life. What we *say* is bound with what we *do*. I feel like saying here: in the beginning was the deed. How can I know what world a lion inhabits? And so how could I possibly hope to understand his language? (Pause) Do I fail to understand him because I can't peer into his mind? Because there is something *behind* his words which I can't grasp? What is going on behind my words when I say: 'This is a very pleasant pineapple'?

> *A young American student puts up his hand.*

Well?

STUDENT   The thought, professor.

WITTGENSTEIN   I see. And what thought lies behind the words: 'This is a very pleasant pineapple'?

> *Amused murmurs from the cognoscenti; they sense the trap set for the student.*

STUDENT   Well, I guess ...

WITTGENSTEIN   What do you 'guess'? (Sardonic emphasis)

STUDENT

Openly flailing; the older men are smiling wryly.

I guess it's ... er ... (Lamely, confessing defeat) ... This is a very pleasant pineapple.

WITTGENSTEIN   Listen to me. We imagine the meaning of what we say as something queer, mysterious, hidden from view. It is as though we are held captive here by a dream of depth. But nothing is hidden; everything is open to view. It is just philosophers who muddy the waters. (Pause) Imagine someone saying: I can *know* what's going on inside me; I can only guess at what's going on inside you. Why is this palpable nonsense?

MOORE   There's nothing in the least nonsensical about it.

WITTGENSTEIN   I see. So you, Moore, can know what's going on inside you?

MOORE   Of course. Suppose I have a pain in my chest. I *know* I do; you can only surmise it.

WITTGENSTEIN

Closing his eyes, then opening them again.

What you have just said strikes me as completely meaningless. As if a man were to say: "But I know how tall I am!', and placed his hand on top of his head.

RUSSELL   Look here, Wittgenstein.

Strikes himself on the chest.

You can't know *this* pain; only I can.

WITTGENSTEIN   You're *sure* that you know it, Russell? You don't *doubt* that you had a pain just then?

RUSSELL   How could I?

WITTGENSTEIN   Then if you can't speak of doubt here, you can't speak of knowledge either.

RUSSELL   I don't follow.

WITTGENSTEIN   It makes no sense to speak of knowing something in a context where we could not possibly doubt it. Therefore, to say 'I know I am in pain' is entirely senseless.

> *We are looking at an elderly white-haired don towards the back of the room. His eyes close, he begins to nod;* WITTGENSTEIN's *voice begins to blur and fade until it becomes mere unintelligible droning. The elderly don wakes with a start as* WITTGENSTEIN's *voice comes back into focus.*

When you want to know the meaning of a word, don't look *inside* yourself; look at the uses of the word in our way of life. Look at how we *behave*. The best picture of the soul is the human body. (Pause) And to do this, we must get rid of the illusions which philosophy breeds. Philosophy leaves everything exactly as it was; it can in no way interfere with our forms of life. It simply assembles reminders of what we knew anyway, but which was too familiar for us to recognise. Otherwise philosophy is just dangerous nonsense and should be given up immediately. (Pause) I'm sorry: you have a worthless teacher today. I'm cleaned out; you must forgive me.

> *Rises; the others get up, fold their deckchairs and begin to leave the room.*

KEYNES

> *Coming over to* WITTGENSTEIN.

That was brilliant, Wittgenstein. Well it must have been, I didn't understand a word.

WITTGENSTEIN   It was frightful.

KEYNES   Well, you certainly made me feel like a vegetable.

WITTGENSTEIN   How could you possibly, Keynes? It doesn't feel like anything to be a vegetable.

MOORE

> *Wandering up, pipe in mouth.*

I just can't see it, Wittgenstein. It somehow just seems natural to say 'I know I'm in pain'.

WITTGENSTEIN   (Dismissively) Oh, natural. Tell me, Moore, why do people say it seems more *natural* to believe that the sun goes round the earth, rather than the other way round?

MOORE   What? Well, obviously, because it *looks* that way.

WITTGENSTEIN

> *To* JARRETT.

Come to a flick with me.

JARRETT   All right.

> *They move to the door and down the staircase.*

INT   STAIRCASE   LATE AFTERNOON

WITTGENSTEIN   Who were those women?

JARRETT   Philosophy students from Girton, I think.

WITTGENSTEIN   You might as well tell them to stay away. I've never met a woman who wasn't an idiot at philosophy.

EXT   TRINITY COLLEGE   LATE AFTERNOON

> WITTGENSTEIN *and* JARRETT *emerge from the staircase into Great Court.*

JARRETT   You don't think Moore had a point?

WITTGENSTEIN   Moore is an interesting example of how far a man can get on absolutely no intelligence whatsoever.

> JARRETT *peers nervously over his shoulder, to ensure* MOORE *isn't within hearing range.*

INT   CINEMA   LATE AFTERNOON

> WITTGENSTEIN *and* JARRETT *are in the front row of a sparsely populated cinema, watching an extremely bad Western.* WITTGENSTEIN *is sitting rigidly upright on the edge of his seat, munching a pork pie, eyes fixed intently on the screen.* JARRETT *is furtively scribbling something on his lap.*

WITTGENSTEIN

> *In a fierce hiss, without taking his eyes from the screen.*

What are you *doing*?

JARRETT   (Whispering) I'm trying to make notes on your class before I forget it.

WITTGENSTEIN   Don't be ridiculous. You'll miss the plot.

JARRETT   There isn't any plot.

WITTGENSTEIN   There might be.

> *Swiping movement with his hand, eyes still glued to screen.*

Put it away; put it away this minute.

JARRETT *abandons his scribbling with a sigh and looks at the screen; we see* WITTGENSTEIN *munching his pie slowly, gaze fixed and staring.*

INT   RUSSELL'S ROOM   EVENING

Loud 20s dance music on a gramophone. RUSSELL *and* DAISY *are dancing an improvised version of the Charleston with extravagant abandon, camping it up, both fairly tipsy. They sip champagne as they jog around; empty bottles litter the room. They treat each other to silly little moues, fluttering gestures of the hands. A loud thumping at the door. The couple continue to dance. The thumping repeated urgently.*

RUSSELL   (Shouting) Hold on a minute.

He and DAISY *dance their way over to the door;* RUSSELL *throws open the door while still cavorting to reveal* WITTGENSTEIN.

WITTGENSTEIN   Russell, I think I'm going to kill myself.

RUSSELL   Right-ho. Half a minute.

Waltzes over to the gramophone and removes arm from record.

Come on in, Wittgenstein, take a pew. Oh sorry, this is Dolly.

DAISY   (Broad Cockney accent) Daisy.

RUSSELL   Daisy. Daisy, this is Ludwig Wittgenstein, the second greatest philosopher of our time. He's Austrian.

WITTGENSTEIN

Bowing stiffly.

How do you do.

DAISY   Oooh, 'e looks ever so clever, doesn't 'e?

RUSSELL

> *To* WITTGENSTEIN.

Champagne?

WITTGENSTEIN   No thank you.

> *Sits in armchair.*

DAISY   What's it all about then, duckie?

WITTGENSTEIN   I beg your pardon?

DAISY

> *With sweep of arm.*

You know, all this. What's it all about then?

RUSSELL

> *Coming over to fill* DAISY's *glass.*

Do leave Dr Wittgenstein alone, dearest heart.

DAISY   I thought you said 'e was a philosopher.

RUSSELL   So he is, so he is.

DAISY

> *Coming across to perch on the arm of* WITT-
> GENSTEIN's *chair, generous display of leg, arm
> round his shoulders.*

Well he can tell me what it's all about then, can't he?

> *Strokes his hair.*

> WITTGENSTEIN *stares rigidly ahead like a man in
> deep shock.*

You've got lovely eyes.

RUSSELL

> *Faintly peeved.*

I'm a philosopher too, you know.

DAISY   Yeah, well there's only one thing *you* think it's about.

RUSSELL   Why don't you nip out and take a look at King's Chapel?

DAISY   I've seen it, it's boring.

RUSSELL

> *Prising her off* WITTGENSTEIN*'s chair.*

Well go and feed the ducks for a couple of hours. Go on, there's a good girl.

> *Pats her on the bottom.*

I'll meet you in the Pig for a drink at nine.

DAISY   Well if you're throwing me out I think I'll take the bubbly with me.

> *Picks up bottle, blows kiss to* WITTGENSTEIN.

Toodle-oo, then. *Love*-ly eyes. Bye, Bertiekins.

> *Exits.*

WITTGENSTEIN   (Disgustedly) Bertiekins!

RUSSELL   It's just a name.

WITTGENSTEIN   How *can* you associate with such a woman? I find your behaviour quite unspeakable.

RUSSELL   Some of us quite like women, Wittgenstein; most of us, in fact.

WITTGENSTEIN   How *could* you take up with a shop-girl?

RUSSELL   Shop-girl?

Snort of laughter.

Oh don't let the accent fool you; she's the daughter of a Viscount, actually. I think she's some sort of relative of mine.

WITTGENSTEIN   (Grimly) Incest to boot.

RUSSELL   Oh come on, old bean, don't be so ornery.

Sits in armchair.

What's all this about killing yourself?

WITTGENSTEIN   I came here tonight to ask you a question, Russell – to ask the meaning of something that's been puzzling me.

RUSSELL   Right-ho, fire away.

WITTGENSTEIN   Russell, what does *this* mean?

Gives sudden V-sign.

RUSSELL

Taken aback for a second, then burst of laughter.

That? Well, er, it's a sort of ... gesture of contempt, I suppose.

WITTGENSTEIN   A cyclist did this to me on Trinity Street. I was crossing the road and almost collided with him. And I thought to myself: that is *language*. That's why I decided there and then to kill myself.

RUSSELL   Hmm. Seems a bit of an overreaction to kill yourself just because somebody gave you a V-sign.

WITTGENSTEIN

> *Holding up two fingers.*

What's the logical structure of this gesture, Russell? An absurd question, of course: it doesn't have one. That means I've spent most of my life groping down a blind alley.

RUSSELL   I'm afraid you'll have to explain a bit more, old fruit.

WITTGENSTEIN   Philosophy hunts for the essence of meaning. There's no such thing: just the way we do things in everyday life. Things like this.

> *Repeats V-sign.*

The college porter knows that, Russell.

RUSSELL   Ah, I see. You mean you've argued yourself out of a job?

WITTGENSTEIN   A college porter, Russell, is simple. What is it to be simple? Is a broom, for example, simple? Or is it complex, composed of a stick and a brush?

RUSSELL   (Amused) You're philosophising again, old chap; you detest philosophy just like a philosopher. You speak like an old roué weary of copulation.

WITTGENSTEIN   The common people have the answers. Philosophy just states what everybody admits. How does philosophy take the measure of *this*?

> *Wiggles his foot suddenly in the air.*

RUSSELL   It isn't supposed to. That's like complaining you can't play a tune on a carrot.

WITTGENSTEIN   Precisely.

RUSSELL   So you think philosophy is useless?

WITTGENSTEIN   Oh no; it serves us as a sort of therapy. When we're bewitched by the lures of language, philosophy can show us the way back to *terra firma*. But it can't speak of anything that's really important.

RUSSELL   What about Aristotle?

WITTGENSTEIN   I haven't read Aristotle. Look: your friend asked about the meaning of life. That's not a stupid question. But you won't find the answer from philosophy.

RUSSELL   Where, then?

WITTGENSTEIN   Tolstoy. Dostoevsky. Schubert. St Matthew.

RUSSELL   I didn't know you were a Christian.

WITTGENSTEIN   I'm not a religious man; I just look at everything from a religious viewpoint. Tell me, Russell: why is there anything at all, rather than just nothing?

RUSSELL   How the hell do I know? I'm a mathematician, not God Almighty.

WITTGENSTEIN   Do you know what I thought to myself when I woke up this morning?

RUSSELL   No, what?

WITTGENSTEIN   I thought to myself: my work consists of two parts, of which one is not written. This part is the important one.

RUSSELL   Well why not just write it then?

WITTGENSTEIN   Of that of which we cannot speak, it is better to remain silent.

RUSSELL

Rising to pour himself a drink.

Well if you're fed up with philosophy, why not go off and do something else?

WITTGENSTEIN   I've tried; I'm not *fit* for anything else.

Rises and comes over to RUSSELL.

Don't you understand, Russell? – my life is rotten; worthless. The only bit of religion I have is the awful guilt of it.

RUSSELL   You're not worthless, Wittgenstein; you just have this ridiculous thirst for perfection. Then you get disgusted with yourself when you can't live up to it.

WITTGENSTEIN   Of course I want to be perfect; don't you?

RUSSELL

With a laugh.

Christ, no.

WITTGENSTEIN   Then I don't see how we can be friends.

RUSSELL   Friends can disagree.

WITTGENSTEIN   (Passionately) Rubbish! Friends can't disagree – not *my* friends. That's ball.

RUSSELL   Balls, Wittgenstein; the word is plural.

WITTGENSTEIN   I don't give an arse what it is.

Walks across room in agitation, then swings round.

Listen: I said just now that I felt like killing myself. That wasn't a joke. (Pause) Three of my brothers took their own lives. Did you know that?

RUSSELL   (Quietly) No, I didn't. I'm sorry to hear it.

WITTGENSTEIN   And I'll tell you this: I've hardly lived a single day – not a single day – when the thought of destroying myself hasn't occurred to me. But it's no good; it wouldn't be the decent thing. If suicide's allowed, then everything's allowed.

RUSSELL   Think of all the music you'd miss.

WITTGENSTEIN   Yes, music. I suppose that helps to keep me going. (Pause) The problem is, Russell ... the problem is that I can't get rid of *this* .

> *Strikes himself on the chest.*

RUSSELL   You mean your shirt?

WITTGENSTEIN   (Withering look) I mean my body. Philosophy is a sickness of the mind – a disease. I must just go off and find some hole to crawl into before I infect too many young men.

RUSSELL   Well, don't crawl off too soon. You can always talk to me, you know.

WITTGENSTEIN   I suppose I can. You have an interesting mind, Russell, despite being English. But I wouldn't exactly call you a soul-mate. On the whole I find you vain, frivolous and rather shallow.

RUSSELL   (Chuckling) Well, I suppose candour's a virtue. Look, come with me into Hall; it'll take your mind off things.

WITTGENSTEIN   You know I never dine in Hall.

RUSSELL   Just once won't do you any harm.

> *Takes two gowns from a hook on his door.*

Here, you can have my spare gown.

> *Throws gown to* WITTGENSTEIN *and begins to put on his own.*

And you can tell me all about Hegel; it'll save me having to read him.

WITTGENSTEIN   I haven't read him either. But I know what the German mind is like.

RUSSELL   Really?

WITTGENSTEIN   Of course; I was born with one.

They exit.

INT   HALL   EVENING

> RUSSELL *and* WITTGENSTEIN *wend their way through the tables of gowned undergraduates eating dinner, towards High Table, where about twenty gowned dons are dining with the* MASTER *presiding at the top of the table. The* BUTLER *ushers them to two empty seats. The* MASTER *stares hard at* WITTGENSTEIN *and beckons the* BUTLER *over, whispering in his ear. The* BUTLER *nods and comes back to* WITTGENSTEIN.

BUTLER   Beg pardon, Dr Wittgenstein, but the Master requests that you would kindly put on your tie.

WITTGENSTEIN   Tie? What tie? I don't have a tie.

BUTLER   Very good, sir.

> *Returns to the* MASTER *and communicates this information in low tones. The* MASTER *eyes* WITTGENSTEIN *frostily, then murmurs again to the* BUTLER. BUTLER *returns to* WITTGENSTEIN. *The* FELLOWS *are now watching these toings-and-froings, like spectators at a tennis game.*

Beg pardon, sir, but the Master asks me to point out that it's customary for Fellows to wear their ties at High Table.

RUSSELL   Oh for God's sake, Lambert, has the Master nothing better to do?

WITTGENSTEIN   But I don't have a tie. I haven't worn a tie since I was ten.

BUTLER   I could fetch one for you, sir.

WITTGENSTEIN   How could I possibly wear someone else's tie?

BUTLER   Very good, sir.

> *Returns to the* MASTER *and whispers.*
>
> *The* FELLOWS *have ceased eating and are following the proceedings with interest. The* MASTER *has a word in the* BUTLER's *ear; the* BUTLER *comes back to* WITTGENSTEIN.

I'm very sorry, Dr Wittgenstein, but the Master requests you to leave the Hall.

RUSSELL   This is intolerable. Stay right where you are, Wittgenstein.

> WITTGENSTEIN *rises to his feet. He looks down the High Table, at the silent ranks of* FELLOWS' *faces turned stonily or inquisitively towards him. He gives an enormous V-sign.*

INT   KING'S CHAPEL   DAY

> *We are looking at the ceiling of the chapel, hearing loud organ music.* WITTGENSTEIN *is lying on his back in a pew, eyes shut tight;* JARRETT *is sitting in the pew behind.* WITTGENSTEIN *accompanies the organ music with perfect whistling; the music ends,* WITTGENSTEIN *sits suddenly upright.*

WITTGENSTEIN   Do you know what that reminded me of?

JARRETT   What?

WITTGENSTEIN   The delightful way the various parts of the body differ in temperature from each other.

JARRETT   You think that's what it's about?

WITTGENSTEIN   Of course not, don't be so idiotic. It just reminded me of it, that's all.

>   *Gets to his feet.*

Let's go and take a walk on the Backs.

>   *They walk out of the chapel.*

EXT   KING'S COLLEGE   DAY

>   WITTGENSTEIN *and* JARRETT *walk through the front court of King's, where undergraduates are lying or sitting on the grass.*

JARRETT   Someone once told me you had seven grand pianos at home in Vienna.

WITTGENSTEIN   Was it really seven? There were a lot, anyway. (Pause) I sometimes think I'd like to write a work of philosophy that sounded just like a symphony; or like a poem. That's the only way one could really do philosophy.

JARRETT   How would anyone understand it?

WITTGENSTEIN   They wouldn't. Its meaning would be inexpressible.

>   *Three* UNDERGRADUATES, *lounging on the grass, watch the two dons pass by.*

1ST UNDERGRADUATE   Hey, that's Wittgenstein!

2ND UNDERGRADUATE   What, old Vitter-Gitter? Which one?

1ST UNDERGRADUATE   The little one.

3RD UNDERGRADUATE   It can't be; he hasn't been out of his room for thirty years.

1ST UNDERGRADUATE   Someone told me he teaches lying on his back wrapped in cardboard.

3RD UNDERGRADUATE   Isn't he a millionaire or something?

2ND UNDERGRADUATE   He was, but he gave it all away. He lives on powdered eggs and he's only got one change of underwear.

1ST UNDERGRADUATE   He's probably still got a few bob stashed away somewhere. Why don't you go over and flutter your eyelashes at him? You might get a hand-out.

> WITTGENSTEIN *and* JARRETT *have reached the river bank, where they sit down.*

JARRETT   Somebody told me you were a mystic. Is that true?

WITTGENSTEIN   You mustn't think it's anything to do with being *holy.*

JARRETT   What's it to do with, then?

WITTGENSTEIN   I used to believe that language gave us a picture of the world.

JARRETT   What's mystical about that?

WITTGENSTEIN   But it can't give us a picture of how it does that. That would be like trying to see yourself seeing something. *How* language does that would be beyond expression. That's the mystical. (Lies back) But that was all wrong. Language isn't a *picture* at all.

JARRETT   What is it, then?

WITTGENSTEIN   It's a tool; an instrument. There isn't just *one* picture of the world; there are lots of different language-games. Different forms of life, different ways of doing things with words; they don't all hang together. (Pause) Speaking of tools, I've fixed you up with a job at the Electrical Instruments Company.

JARRETT   (Startled) What?

WITTGENSTEIN   I had a word with the manager; you start as an engineering apprentice on Monday.

JARRETT   Really?

WITTGENSTEIN   What's the matter?

JARRETT   (Rueful chuckle) Well you might have consulted me.

WITTGENSTEIN   (Tetchily) We talked about it. I thought you'd be pleased.

JARRETT   Well I don't know. It's going to be hard, leaving all this.

> *Waves arms around.*

WITTGENSTEIN   No it won't; you'll be doing something useful.

JARRETT   You used to be an engineer yourself, didn't you?

WITTGENSTEIN   I should have stuck to it. You should work with your hands.

> *Takes one of* JARRETT's *hands in his own.*

You have fine, strong hands. You ought to create with them.

> *They lie silently on the grass together.* WITTGEN-STEIN *retains* JARRETT's *hand in his own.*

INT   GARAGE   DAY

> *A sudden deafening noise of engines. A few work-men in overalls are at work repairing bicycles and motor cycles. A young burly* MECHANIC *is bent low over a motor cycle he is repairing, face streaked with oil and sweat. The garage door is*

open; WITTGENSTEIN *peers cautiously round it. He catches the* MECHANIC's *eye, then gestures with his head. The* MECHANIC *indicates the presence of the other workmen with a gesture of his head.* WITTGENSTEIN *nods and retires. After a pause the* MECHANIC *stops work, wipes his hands, and saunters to the door.*

EXT   OUTSIDE GARAGE   DAY

WITTGENSTEIN   (Low voice) I thought you might like to come to tea.

MECHANIC   All right. When?

WITTGENSTEIN   Sunday – at four. In my rooms.

MECHANIC   OK.

Goes back into garage; we see WITTGENSTEIN's *face in close-up, tense, straining.*

EXT   MEADOW   DAY

We are looking at a large, open expanse of meadow. Suddenly WITTGENSTEIN *comes into view, running hard, and passes out of it again. This is repeated three or four times. We pull back a little: now* MOORE *appears, running, puffing hard, apparently circling* WITTGENSTEIN. *The two men appear and disappear from sight, with* MOORE *in the foreground. We pull back more;* MRS MOORE, *walking briskly, comes into view, wearing a new coat with a row of buttons down the front.* MOORE *is circling her at a trot, and* WITTGENSTEIN *is circling* MOORE.

They are playing the planet game: MRS MOORE *as the sun,* MOORE *as the earth,* WITTGENSTEIN

> *as the moon, the whole configuration moving*
> *steadily across the meadow.*

WITTGENSTEIN   (Shouting) Keep it up, Moore! Come on, man, speed it up!

MOORE   (Shouting back) I'm going as fast as I can.

WITTGENSTEIN   You're slowing the whole thing down!

MRS MOORE   (Shouting) Should I go faster, Ludwig?

WITTGENSTEIN   No, no, keep going as you are. Come on, Moore, keep it up, keep it up.

MOORE

> *Sinking to the ground.*

I'm done for.

> WITTGENSTEIN *and* MRS MOORE *come to a halt;*
> WITTGENSTEIN *comes and bends sternly over the*
> *deflated* MOORE.

WITTGENSTEIN   You've ruined everything! We were just getting into rhythm.

MOORE   (Sulkily) Oh go and play with somebody else.

WITTGENSTEIN   All right, you can be the sun this time – it's easier. You be the sun, I'll be the earth, and she can be the moon.

> *Shouts to* MRS MOORE.

You can be the moon this time!

MRS MOORE   (Shouting back) I think we should take a rest. You said you had a visitor back at college.

WITTGENSTEIN   (Consulting watch) So I have.

> *To* MOORE, *in consolatory tone.*

All right, Moore, I'll let you be the sun next time.

MOORE   Humph.

MRS MOORE

> *Approaching* WITTGENSTEIN

Oh, before you go, Ludwig: you haven't admired my new coat.

> *Twirls a little.*

What do you think?

WITTGENSTEIN   Hmm. It could be better.

MRS MOORE   (Deflated) Oh, really?

WITTGENSTEIN

> *Eyeing coat carefully.*

Yes, it could definitely be improved. Stand perfectly still.

> *Puts hand in pocket and produces a claspknife, which he opens.*

MRS MOORE   Ludwig, what on earth are you doing?

WITTGENSTEIN   I said stand perfectly still!

> *Appraises coat.*

Ah yes.

> *Makes sudden lunge at the coat with his knife.*

MOORE   Wittgenstein, what the devil do you think you're up to?

> WITTGENSTEIN *cuts all the buttons off the coat;* MRS MOORE *gives faint scream.*

WITTGENSTEIN   Keep *still*, I tell you!

Finishes cutting off buttons.

There now.

Steps back a pace.

What do you think of that, Moore?

MOORE

Who has staggered indignantly to his feet.

What do I think? My God, man, I think it's a bloody ... (Looks at wife) ... I think it's a bloody ... sight better, that's what I think.

MRS MOORE   (Looking down) Do you know, I do believe you're right.

> WITTGENSTEIN *pockets his knife with a smile of triumph.*

INT   WITTGENSTEIN'S ROOM   DAY

> WITTGENSTEIN *is pouring out tea dressed only in his dressing gown. We are looking at him from the viewpoint of the* MECHANIC, *only the back of whose head is visible from behind his armchair. There is a deckchair in front of the armchair, for* WITTGENSTEIN's *use.*

WITTGENSTEIN   Have some tea.

> *We see the* MECHANIC *from in front; he is dressed only in his underpants.*

MECHANIC   Ta.

WITTGENSTEIN   Help yourself to some cake. It's very good cake; my sister Leopoldine sends it to me from Austria.

MECHANIC   (Looking round) You could do with a bit more furniture in this place.

WITTGENSTEIN   I don't like clutter.

Sits in deckchair.

MECHANIC   I could pick you up some second-hand if you want.

WITTGENSTEIN   I like places to be sparse. I built a house once for my sister, in Vienna, just like that.

MECHANIC   You built a house?

WITTGENSTEIN   Well, I designed it.

MECHANIC   I thought you'd have more books.

WITTGENSTEIN   I don't have much use for books.

MECHANIC   Neither do I. (Pause) I thought that was your job, like.

WITTGENSTEIN   My job is to think. I read detective thrillers, mostly.

MECHANIC   Me too. (Pause) What are you thinking about at the moment?

WITTGENSTEIN   I don't think you'd understand.

MECHANIC   Give us a try.

WITTGENSTEIN

Pause; eyes him warily.

All right: I'll give you a try. (Pause) For many years now, a certain picture of things has held philosophy captive. At the centre of this picture is the lonely human soul, brooding over its private experiences: experiences which are thought to be unique and incommunicable. This individual is a prisoner of his own body; and he is locked out from contact with others by the walls of *their* bodies, which render them mysterious and opaque to him. I want to overthrow this picture.

There is no private meaning: we are what we are only because we share a common language, and common forms of life. Philosophy has moved on the pure ice of logic; but I take us back to the rough ground of our social practices.

> *We see the* MECHANIC's *face: empty, uncomprehending.*

But of course, beyond all that, there still lies the inexpressible: that which we must not say.

MECHANIC   You mean like swearing and stuff?

WITTGENSTEIN   I mean like art, ethics, religion. (Pause) Well? Did you understand all that?

MECHANIC   Nothing.

> *A knock at the door.* WITTGENSTEIN *leaps up in alarm.*

Who's that?

WITTGENSTEIN   I don't know; get in the bedroom. Go on, get in the bedroom.

> MECHANIC *rises and moves to bedroom.*

Put your clothes on. It's alright, I'll get rid of him.

> MECHANIC *disappears into the bedroom;* WITTGENSTEIN *opens the door to reveal* RUSSELL.

RUSSELL

> *Eyeing* WITTGENSTEIN's *dressing gown.*

Sleeping late?

WITTGENSTEIN   (Flustered) Oh Russell – do come in.

> *Looks nervously over his shoulder;* RUSSELL *enters the room.*

RUSSELL   (Pacing, angry) I've just been talking to David Jarrett. What the hell do you think you're playing at, Wittgenstein?

WITTGENSTEIN   What do you mean?

RUSSELL   I mean all this poppycock about the Electrical Instruments Company.

WITTGENSTEIN   What about it?

RUSSELL   What about it? You've just persuaded the most brilliant mathematician Trinity's had for a quarter of a century to commit intellectual suicide, that's all.

WITTGENSTEIN   I persuaded him into nothing; it was his own decision.

RUSSELL   That's rubbish, Wittgenstein; what do you think his parents are going to say?

WITTGENSTEIN   (Frostily) I haven't the foggiest.

RUSSELL   Jarrett's parents are working people – his father's a railwayman. They've sacrificed everything to get him to Cambridge.

WITTGENSTEIN   What could they possibly know about it?

RUSSELL   They know everything about it! They're experts in what it's like to work a twelve-hour shift for two-pence-ha' penny.

WITTGENSTEIN   I'm afraid I could never come to terms with this side of you, Russell.

RUSSELL   Which side?

WITTGENSTEIN   Left-wing politics.

RUSSELL   That has absolutely nothing to do with it.

WITTGENSTEIN   Oh really? I heard you'd become patron of some new League; I forget the title.

RUSSELL   The Women's League of Peace and Freedom, if you want to know.

WITTGENSTEIN   My God!

RUSSELL   I suppose you'd prefer the All-Male League of War and Slavery.

WITTGENSTEIN   Better that! Better that!

RUSSELL   Look, Wittgenstein, Jarrett's parents are workers – stout peasant folk, sons of the soil. That's what you're supposed to admire – when it's confined to the pages of Tolstoy, that is. When you can't romanticise it from your college room. Your problem, old bean, is that you can't decide whether you're mystic or a mechanic.

WITTGENSTEIN   I've never met David's parents.

RUSSELL   I'd strongly advise you not to. Can't you see what you're doing? You're foisting your own self-hatred onto him.

WITTGENSTEIN   Russell, I fear you may have been reading Sigmund Freud.

RUSSELL   What of it?

WITTGENSTEIN   It's dangerous stuff, take my word for it. It takes one Viennese to know another.

RUSSELL   Freud's nothing to do with it. You can't stand dons, so having young Jarrett sweat it out in some godawful factory offers you a vicarious escape. You can't *do* that to people, Wittgenstein; you can't use them as fodder for your own fantasies.

WITTGENSTEIN   What I do is no business of yours.

RUSSELL   It's my business to stop you from – what was the word you used? – infecting too many young men. You have a terrible power over them, don't you see that? Half of Cambridge goes round imitating your mannerisms; there are Wittgenstein mimics in every bloody teashop.

WITTGENSTEIN   You know I've never encouraged disciples.

RUSSELL   I'm talking about *you*, not your ideas. You lord it over others and you don't even know it. All aristocrats idealise the common folk – as long as they keep stoking the boilers. I should know; I was brought up like that too.

WITTGENSTEIN   That was a long time ago – in another country.

RUSSELL   No it wasn't; you don't step out of that sort of background like slipping out of a dinner jacket. You're not a peasant, Wittgenstein: your father was one of the richest industrialists in Austria, you were born in a house bigger than the Albert Hall and Johannes Brahms used to drop round for tea. All right, so you gave all your money away; Jarrett isn't that privileged. You gave it away because you have to strip yourself to nothing; look at this room. Why do you detest yourself so much?

WITTGENSTEIN

Going to the door and opening it.

Russell, I would like to say that our friendship is now over. I don't think we should ever speak to each other again.

RUSSELL   Have you the faintest conception of what trying to be your friend is like? You demand more devotion than the Virgin Mary. You clamour for love like a greedy child – and when you get it you haven't a clue what to do with it.

WITTGENSTEIN

Still holding open door.

If you'd just return to me sometime the various items I've loaned you ...

RUSSELL   Oh do sit down, Wittgenstein, for Christ's sake. Don't be such an ass.

WITTGENSTEIN   How can I possibly speak to a man who believes I corrupt others?

RUSSELL   I was only quoting your own words.

WITTGENSTEIN   Russell, I can never speak to you again unless you take that back.

RUSSELL   I'll gladly take it back; I didn't use the word 'corrupt' anyway.

WITTGENSTEIN   You unreservedly withdraw the accusation that I'm a corrupter of youth?

RUSSELL   Of course I do.

WITTGENSTEIN

> *Closing the door.*

Then I accept your apology.

> *The* MECHANIC *knocks tentatively on the inside of the bedroom door.*

RUSSELL

> *With a start.*

What's that?

WITTGENSTEIN   What?

RUSSELL   There's somebody in there.

> *The* MECHANIC *knocks louder.*

WITTGENSTEIN   What do you mean?

RUSSELL   There's somebody in your bedroom.

WITTGENSTEIN   (Feebly) Don't be so ridiculous. Look here, Russell, I think you'd better go.

Another knock.

I have to ... ah ... have to see someone ...

RUSSELL

Shielding WITTGENSTEIN *with his body.*

Keep back, Wittgenstein.

Calls out loudly.

Who's there? Come on out!

The bedroom door opens slowly, to reveal the MECHANIC, *now fully dressed.*

MECHANIC

To WITTGENSTEIN

Sorry mate, I've got to go.

Nods to RUSSELL.

Hello there. Thanks for the tea then. Cheers.

The MECHANIC *walks to the door.* RUSSELL *stares with astonishment at* WITTGENSTEIN. WITTGEN-STEIN *stares intently at the carpet.*

EXT   TRINITY COLLEGE   DAY

KEYNES is striding through Great Court towards the foot of WITTGENSTEIN's *staircase.*

INT   WITTGENSTEIN'S ROOM   DAY

> WITTGENSTEIN *is playing the clarinet, a passage from Mozart's Clarinet Concerto, with impressive skill.*

INT   STAIRCASE   DAY

> KEYNES *mounts the staircase, takes a deckchair from the pile outside the door, and knocks on the door. Throughout this the sounds of* WITTGEN-STEIN*'s clarinet.*

INT   WITTGENSTEIN'S ROOM   DAY

WITTGENSTEIN

> *Laying down the clarinet.*

Come in!

> KEYNES *enters, carrying deckchair.*

KEYNES   My dear fellow, don't let me stop you. I'll just sit here and listen.

WITTGENSTEIN   Oh, that was atrocious. I'm bungling everything today. Let me get you something, Keynes.

KEYNES

> *Setting up deckchair and sitting in it.*

Well, you don't have a stiff Scotch, of course, and I won't be palmed off with cocoa.

WITTGENSTEIN   I had a fearful row with Russell yesterday. He said I was an evil influence.

KEYNES   Oh, I'm sure you must be exaggerating.

WITTGENSTEIN   Well, he may be right. I've lain awake all night thinking about it.

KEYNES   What's worrying you, Wittgenstein; your logic or your sins?

WITTGENSTEIN   Both; my sins, mostly.

KEYNES   Well I'm hardly a shining example of moral virtue myself.

WITTGENSTEIN   (Coldly) I never imagined you were. (Pause) You know, Keynes, people sometimes think I behave strangely. They're like someone who looks through a window and can't explain the odd behaviour of a passer-by. They don't know that a storm is raging out there, and that the man is keeping his feet only with the greatest difficulty. Do you understand what it means to live like that?

KEYNES   No, I can't say I do.

WITTGENSTEIN   (Low voice) Every day, every hour, every moment, I keep my feet with the greatest of difficulty. And the slightest gust of dishonesty would be enough to bowl me over forever. But of course, not deceiving oneself is quite impossible.

KEYNES   Do you want my diagnosis, Wittgenstein? Remembering, of course, that I speak as a card-carrying immoralist.

WITTGENSTEIN   All right.

KEYNES   I think you're suffering from a potentially terminal case of moral integrity. We're all wilting in the glare of your remorseless honesty. If you just allowed yourself to be a bit more sinful there might be hope yet for your salvation.

WITTGENSTEIN   Salvation is the only thing that concerns me. But Keynes, there may not be much I can be sure of, but of one thing I'm certain: we are not here to have a good time.

KEYNES   Spoken like a true Protestant. (Pause) Let me tell you a little story. There was once a young man who dreamed of reducing the world to pure logic. And because he was a very clever young man, he actually managed to do it. And when he had finished, he stood back and admired his handiwork. It was beautiful: a world purged of imperfection and indeterminacy, like countless acres of gleaming ice stretching silently to the horizon. Each object in this world sparkled in the purity of its being, each thing cleanly demarcated from its neighbours. So the clever young man looked around at the new world he had created, and decided to set out and explore it. He took one step forward, and fell flat on his back. You see, he had forgotten about *friction*. The ice was smooth and level and stainless, but you couldn't walk there. So the young man sat down and viewed his marvellous creation and wept bitter tears. And after some years had passed, he grew up into a wise old man who came to understand that roughness and ambiguity and indeterminacy aren't imperfections – they're what make things work. He wanted to run and dance; so he had to dig up all those gleaming acres of ice until he discovered the rough ground beneath them. And the words and things scattered up on this ground were all battered and tarnished and ambiguous; and the wise old man saw that this was the way things were. But something in him was still homesick for the ice, where everything was radiant and absolute and relentless. And so, though he liked the *idea* of the rough ground, he couldn't bring himself to live there. So now he was marooned between earth and ice, at home in neither; and this was the cause of all his grief.

    Pause.

WITTGENSTEIN   I'm thinking of going away.

KEYNES   Where to this time? Not the Soviet Union again, I hope.

WITTGENSTEIN   What's wrong with the Soviet Union?

KEYNES   My dear fellow, the place is one enormous labour camp.

WITTGENSTEIN   There's nothing wrong with labour.

KEYNES   There is if they shoot you for not doing it.

WITTGENSTEIN   I'm thinking of going to Ireland. A friend of mine has a cottage on the Galway coast.

KEYNES   That's good. In Ireland they shoot you if you *do* work.

Moves to the door.

Well, send me a postcard.

WITTGENSTEIN   Keynes.

KEYNES

Turning at the door.

Yes?

WITTGENSTEIN   You didn't say how that story of yours ended.

KEYNES   I don't know yet; I'm really not sure of very much. But there's one thing I am certain of: we *are* here to have a good time.

Smiles, exit. Fade out on WITTGENSTEIN*'s face.*

EXT   BEACH   DAY

WITTGENSTEIN*'s walking on the beach near his Irish cottage. Irish music.*

EXT   COTTAGE   DAY

> WITTGENSTEIN *is sitting in the window of his cottage, scribbling notes. Music again. He looks up and gazes out of the window.*

EXT   COTTAGE   DAY

> KEYNES *drives up to the cottage.* WITTGENSTEIN *is working at the window.* KEYNES *gets out of his car.*

KEYNES

> *Seeing* WITTGENSTEIN.

Wittgenstein!

> WITTGENSTEIN *disappears from the window and appears at the cottage door.*

WITTGENSTEIN   Keynes! My dear fellow, you came.

> *They meet and shake hands outside the cottage.*

KEYNES   It's wonderful to see you; I came as soon as I got your wire. My God, it's taken me the best part of two days to find this bloody place.

WITTGENSTEIN   Well, here you see me in my fastness.

KEYNES   I'll say; this must be remote enough even for you.

WITTGENSTEIN   Come in; I've got the kettle on.

> *They walk to the cottage door.*

KEYNES   The organic society at last, hey?

WITTGENSTEIN   I'm not sure about that. The dogs are a

nuisance – keep me awake at night. but I've managed to tame some birds.

KEYNES   Really?

WITTGENSTEIN   Just a few. They come to be fed in the mornings.

KEYNES   St Ludwig of Assisi.

> *They pass into the cottage.*

INT   COTTAGE   DAY

WITTGENSTEIN   Sit down; I'll just brew the tea.

> *Goes into kitchen.*

KEYNES

> *Wandering around living room, looking at* WITT-GENSTEIN's *notes on his desk.*

How's work going?

> *Shouting into kitchen.*

WITTGENSTEIN   (Shouting back) It's creeping along.

KEYNES   (Shouting) Well, knowing you that means you've just penned a couple of masterpieces.

> *He continues to poke around the living room; after a while* WITTGENSTEIN *emerges from the kitchen with a tray of tea things.*

WITTGENSTEIN   Here we are.

> *Places tray on table.*

How's Cambridge?

KEYNES   Oh come on, whenever did it change? What about you? What's the news from the medicine man?

WITTGENSTEIN   Not too good, I'm afraid. I saw a specialist in Dublin last week; it's cancer of the prostate gland.

KEYNES

> *After a pause.*

My dear good fellow.

WITTGENSTEIN   It's early stages yet; and it responds to hormone therapy, so they say. I could live for years.

KEYNES   What can I do?

WITTGENSTEIN   You can take me back to Cambridge. I don't want to die here.

KEYNES   As soon as you like.

WITTGENSTEIN   You mustn't think I'm afraid of dying Keynes. It's death that gives meaning to life – gives it its shape. Anyway, I've never felt that I had any right to live in the first place.

KEYNES   Who needs a right?

WITTGENSTEIN   It's odd: when I was in the trenches I always used to ask them to transfer me to more dangerous locations. They found it awfully confusing at headquarters. I just hoped that somehow being near to death might bring some light into my life.

KEYNES   And you didn't fear being killed?

WITTGENSTEIN   Not really. I had this queer feeling that whatever actually happened to me I couldn't be basically harmed. That my life was somehow ... hidden away; unassailable. Do you know that feeling?

KEYNES   I can't say I do.

WITTGENSTEIN   It's at the root of the religious sense. I

suppose you might say that I'm a believer in everything but the premises.

KEYNES   You mean the existence of God?

WITTGENSTEIN   Yes: that sort of minor detail.

They both laugh.

KEYNES   They told me you were decorated for bravery in the war.

WITTGENSTEIN   The war changed me forever. It was like standing on the very limits of language, with the darkness of death at my back – and being struck dumb.

KEYNES   But you don't believe there's anything beyond those limits?

WITTGENSTEIN   Maybe there is; something moving somewhere in the darkness. But if there is, then it's un-speakable. You can't say it, only show it – like a smile or a kiss.

KEYNES   Well, it's good to hear you're still writing.

WITTGENSTEIN   Yes, it's coming together slowly. Who knows, I might even have written something half-decent over here. But if I have, it's not for this age. I'm not at home in the twentieth century, Keynes; I won't be sorry to say goodbye to it. We're moving into the dark ages, you know.

KEYNES   Mr Hitler's a bit of a worry.

WITTGENSTEIN   I know; I was at school with him. He was a revolting little runt even then.

Pours some tea for KEYNES.

Here, have some tea. I'm ready to go back any time. Would you like to rest first?

KEYNES   *Taking tea cup.*

No, ready when you are.

WITTGENSTEIN   I'll just go and say goodbye to the sea.

Moves to the door, exits.

EXT   COTTAGE   DAY

WITTGENSTEIN comes through the door of the cottage, and stares at the sea. Irish lament, played on the pipes. KEYNES comes through the cottage door, carrying WITTGENSTEIN's suitcase.

KEYNES   (Shouting) All set?

KEYNES puts the suitcase in the car; they both climb in.

INT   CAR   DAY

WITTGENSTEIN is looking out at the scenery.

WITTGENSTEIN   You know, I'd quite like to compose a philosophical work which consisted entirely of jokes. (Pause) But I doubt I could pull it off.

KEYNES   Why not?

WITTGENSTEIN   I don't have much sense of humour.

They continue to drive along, WITTGENSTEIN still looking out. Fade out.

THIS IS NOT A FILM OF LUDWIG WITTGENSTEIN

Derek Jarman

Philosophy and Film. Words and Images. There are no words in a camera. A camera is silent.

Ludwig believed language was a series of pictures. Later, when he had watched too many films, he abandoned this notion.

What might a picture of green be? Which green? Munsell was making a colour chart to codify colour for government and industry, but that explained nothing.

Ludwig looked back past this attempt to fix colour. Others had described green. Was green Venusian? Cool and moist as the neoplatonist Ficino maintained.

A 'handbag' was a handbag. But what of 'because'? What picture did that bring to mind?

He noted that he read colour into a black and white photo. White had not been white since Newton discovered the Spectrum. White is colour full.

The boy in the photo was blonde. Ludwig knew that. Was he wearing a red dress? Did he imagine the red dress in the achromatic greys? Colour glimmered in the mind's eye. Nothing was quite what it seemed. It was another language.

'Shadow is the Queen of Colour', said Aristotle. Ludwig

said, 'What can we possibly learn from him?' Ludwig was no schoolman.

The forward exploration of Colour is Queer. Leonardo in his notebook, Newton's *Optics* and Ludwig's *Remarks on Colour*. Goethe is wrong-headed and saved only by a sharp pen.

Remarks on Colour was a path for me back to the *Tractatus*.

What is a picture of Queer? There is no one picture.

Leonardo experimented with colours and boys. He looked the world in the face. Ludwig and Newton shared a repression. Isaac worked without stop. Ludwig found a black hole in his words. For this there was no language.

He was uncomfortable with his sexuality, yet could not believe he was not a part of the world. 'The world is everything that is the case.'

Ludwig was locked up by denial. Every now and then he bolted to Norway or Ireland.

He faced his buried Jewish ancestry. He had to save his sisters from the death camps.

But wrote, 'Even the greatest Jewish Thinker is no more than talented.'

Ludwig said, 'How can I be myself?' That is modern.

Ludwig lives in a post-Copernican world. Where he and you are the centre of your respective languages. Language has become a bouquet. There is no true path.

But the ceremonies of everyday language are stuck in Aristotelian flat earth power, institutions. We think erroneously that we have arrived. That there is somewhere to go.

I explore Wittgenstein through Newton's prism: his 'glasse works'. It is through transparency that the world is discovered. The camera lens.

'I want to get rid of the age old picture of the soul brooding in isolation,' said Ludwig. He wanted a public discourse.

What would he have made of computer languages?

And logic. What logic was there in the twentieth century?

The media fights the word and wins as the new century dawns. Are you not as suspicious as I of the vacant images that fill the screen each evening?

There is little or no logic in the media.

Ludwig steered away from himself.

He died of cancer of the prostate – the most unexplored of the erogenous zones.

Serendipity. I had thought of making a film of Ludwig some years ago. 'Loony Ludwig in the Green Valleys of Silliness.' Then Tariq rang.

We had a ten-day shoot for fifty minutes on TV. A week or so into pre-production, the BFI threw down a challenge. Some more cash for a seventy-two minute film.

Ken and I wrote the script to make this film. The Saturdays went out the window. So did October locations in Cambridge. We had to shoot six minutes of cut film a day in a small studio in Waterloo.

Black drapes and cheap remarkable colour. Always the same suit or dress, but the colour changing.

Grey Ludwig and dotty Cambridge, friends in High Key.

Are you coming to the Palladium tonight, Ludwig?

The film had a cast and crew of friends who worked hard and happily together. And excellent catering. Did I hear Fortnum and Mason?

The floors and walls of the small studio draped like a funeral. A black infinity. The minimum of props and settings. Blues, reds, violets. There is one moment of set dressing. Break your own rule.

The film was pared away. I was always removing things. It is the same with the soundtrack. A process of elimination.

Mark of the Naif? No distinction between Bertie, a table, and a rhinoceros. All alive and equal.

Invisible worlds brought into focus. Galileo's telescope. Newton's prism. The glass. Negative. The lens of the Hubble telescope and the camera lens.

Quark, Charm and Strangeness – aka Mr Green – holds a glass to the film. He reflects light back into the lens.

The earnest child becomes the unhappy adult.

Ariel becomes a philosopher. Karl thought himself into the part -Ludwig trapped in a cage, Ariel in a glass cabinet. 'Is there more toil?' When *The Tempest* wrapped, Karl asked Heathcote to release him.

A philosophy of Film. Have no plan. Then you can allow your collaborators to take over.

If you have to say no, do it gently so those around imagine you have said yes.

As the film falls apart, gather up your mistakes and treasure them.

Chaos Theory. You cannot fall into unreason.

Who cares about film. Well I never did. I feel for film the same as Ludwig felt about philosophy. There are more pressing things.

Never go to the cinema unless it is Dreyer's *The Passion of Joan of Arc.*

The cinema was Ludwig's escape. Mine, a garden.

Oh Cambridge, Cambridge, Cambridge.

I have much of Ludwig in me. Not in my work, but in my life.

My film does not portray or betray Ludwig. It is there to open up. It is logic.

And the black? The black annihilates the decorative and concentrates so my characters shine in it like red dwarfs – and green giants. Yellow lines and blue stars.

WITTGENSTEIN

THE DEREK JARMAN FILM

PRE-TITLE SEQUENCE:

YOUNG WITTGENSTEIN *sits behind his desk writing. We hear him mumble what he writes.*

YOUNG WITTGENSTEIN   People ... did ... not ... sometimes ... silly things ... nothing intelligent ... ever get done.

He puts down his pen and looks directly at camera.

YOUNG WITTGENSTEIN   If people did not sometimes do silly things, nothing intelligent would ever get done.

SC. 1   FAMILY PHOTOCALL

YOUNG WITTGENSTEIN bounces up in frame dressed in Roman fancy dress. The sound of an orchestra tuning up.

YOUNG WITTGENSTEIN   Hello. My name is Ludwig Wittgenstein. I'm a prodigy. I'm going to tell you my story. I was born in 1889 to a filthy rich family in Vienna. I would like to introduce them to you.

This is my mother Leopoldine. She was crazy about music. In fact, she was so busy entertaining Brahms and Mahler that we were left with the twenty-six tutors and seven grand pianos. Hermine, my oldest sister, was an amateur painter and Gretyl married an American and was psychoanalysed by Freud. Of Helene we will remain silent.

Three of my brothers died young. Hans ran away to America to escape Dad and disappeared off a boat in Chesapeake Bay. Kurt's troops rebelled in the First World War and the shame drove him to suicide. Rudolf, who was bent, spent most of his time in Berlin. When he wasn't being theatrical, he hung out at the Scientific Humanitarian Committee. He topped himself drinking a glass of cyanide in his favourite bar.

That leaves Paul. He was a concert pianist but lost an arm in the war. Ravel composed the Concerto for the Left Hand especially for him.

And as for Dad – he was always in the office investing in American Bonds – that's how we escaped inflation and stayed rich. Mega-rich like the Rockefellers.

> PAUL *begins to play Brahms on the piano. His family looks on – enjoying the solo concert. We fade to credits.*

CHANNEL FOUR TELEVISION

AND

THE BRITISH FILM INSTITUTE

IN ASSOCIATION WITH

UPLINK (Japan)

PRESENT

A BANDUNG PRODUCTION

OF

A DEREK JARMAN FILM

WITTGENSTEIN

WITH

KARL JOHNSON

MICHAEL GOUGH

TILDA SWINTON

JOHN QUENTIN

KEVIN COLLINS
and
CLANCY CHASSAY

NABIL SHABAN

SALLY DEXTER

LYNN SEYMOUR

Written by

DEREK JARMAN

TERRY EAGLETON

KEN BUTLER

Produced by

TARIQ ALI

Directed by

DEREK JARMAN

SC. 2

> YOUNG WITTGENSTEIN *looks up from his desk and notebook.*

YOUNG WITTGENSTEIN   The horrors of hell can be experienced in a single day. That's plenty of time.

SC. 3   BLACK TUTORIAL

> SIX TUTORS *surround* YOUNG WITTGENSTEIN *who is using his sewing machine. They begin simultaneously whispering from his philosophy, getting louder and louder, driving him to shut his eyes and cover his ears in despair.*

YOUNG WITTGENSTEIN (VO)   I was to spend a lifetime disentangling myself from my education. Quite the best to be had in Vienna, Mum said. I shared a history teacher with Adolf Hitler – what a school!!!

SC. 4   YELLOW STAR

> YOUNG WITTGENSTEIN *stands before a blackboard covered in yellow Stars of David. He holds a cane and pretends to gun down the tutors.*

SC. 5   SIGNPOSTS

> YOUNG WITTGENSTEIN *stands by the signpost pointing to Manchester. He takes off his glasses and speaks directly to camera.*

YOUNG WITTGENSTEIN   If someone is merely ahead of time, it will catch them up one day.

SC. 6   RED PILLAR BOX

> YOUNG WITTGENSTEIN *walks up to a red post box. He taps it.*

YOUNG WITTGENSTEIN   I am in England, everything around me tells me so.

MARTIAN   Tell me how you are searching and I'll tell you what you're searching for.

> YOUNG WITTGENSTEIN *imagines the voice to come from within the post box. He jumps with surprise at seeing the Martian.*

YOUNG WITTGENSTEIN   Who's that?

MARTIAN   Hail Earthling!

YOUNG WITTGENSTEIN   Earthling? I'm a philosopher, Ludwig Wittgenstein. Who are you?

MARTIAN   You could call me Mr Green. May I ask you a question? How many toes do philosophers have?

YOUNG WITTGENSTEIN   Ten.

MARTIAN   Fascinating – that's how many humans have.

YOUNG WITTGENSTEIN   Mr Green, philosophers are human, and know how many toes they have.

MARTIAN   Oh dear, does that mean Martians can't be philosophers?

YOUNG WITTGENSTEIN   Oh god.

> *He rubs his forehead in disbelief.*

SC. 7   FLYING IN MANCHESTER

> OLDER WITTGENSTEIN *wearing kite wings picks up two lawn mower sprinklers and holds them out like the propellers of a plane. The light catches the swirling water like a Catherine wheel.*

YOUNG WITTGENSTEIN (VO)   I escaped the family by going to Manchester University.

Manchester. An industrial town in the English north. I remember my father saying 'where there's muck, there's brass'. My aim was to be a pioneer in aeronautics, but my experiments ended in a teenage failure and I gave up. I abandoned my unsuccessful attempt to design an engine and like the English hero Dick Whittington, went south to Cambridge to study philosophy with Bertrand Russell.

The water pressure is turned off.

SC. 8   THE RHINO

> WITTGENSTEIN *and* RUSSELL *are sitting at a table in the middle of a heated conversation.* RUSSELL *is frustrated.*

RUSSELL   Why won't you just admit there's no rhinoceros in this room?

WITTGENSTEIN   Because, Professor Russell, the world is made up of facts not things.

RUSSELL   Look for yourself.

> RUSSELL *looks under the table and we see there is nothing there.*

I tell you for a fact – There is no rhinoceros in this room.

WITTGENSTEIN   The issue is metaphysical not empirical.

RUSSELL   I thought the next big step in philosophy would be yours – now I am not so sure.

> RUSSELL *exits with* WITTGENSTEIN *following. We see* YOUNG WITTGENSTEIN *crawling out from beneath the table wearing a yellow rhinoceros horn.*

WITTGENSTEIN   Professor Russell, Professor Russell ...

> YOUNG WITTGENSTEIN *comes out from under*

the table and creeps up towards the camera. He puts his finger to his lips.

YOUNG WITTGENSTEIN   Ssh!

SC. 9   WRITING LETTERS

This scene is cut back and forth between images of RUSSELL writing letters at his gold desk and OTTOLINE MORRELL reading them in bed. She wears a shocking pink ostrich feather hat and eats heart shaped chocolates.

RUSSELL   Dear Ottoline, Herr Sinckel-Winkel hard at it on universals and particulars. He has the pure intellectual passion in the highest degree and it makes me love him. He says that every morning he begins his work with hope, and that every evening he ends in despair.

OTTOLINE   We both have the same feeling that one must understand or die. He is the young man one hopes for. His disposition is that of the artist, intuitive and moody. He affects me, just as I affect you. I get to know every turn and twist of the ways in which I irritate and depress you from watching how ...

RUSSELL   ... he irritates and depresses me. And at the same time I love and admire him. His boiling passion may drive him anywhere.

SC. 10   GILBERT & SULLIVAN

YOUNG WITTGENSTEIN sits on a bright red sofa. He clinks two cocktail glasses – takes a sip from each and whispers to the camera.

YOUNG WITTGENSTEIN   God the English are a queer bunch. Lady Ottoline Morrell was the queerest. She was fucking the gardener and Russell. All the fun was in the

country houses. Everyone else was miserable. Cambridge was miserable. There was no oxygen there. (Gasp) Can you imagine spending your evenings with those pretentious Apostles. I was no fun at parties. The drunken chit-chat of British intellectuals bored me. So in desperation I fled to Norway and built a small house on a fjord at the end of the world. I started to write 'Notes on Logic'.

SC.11   NORWAY

> WITTGENSTEIN *is rowing his boat on a fjord at night. He is lit by a paraffin lamp. He stops rowing and leans back in his boat.*

WITTGENSTEIN   How can I be a logician before I'm a human being? The most important thing is to settle accounts with myself. It's much easier here in Norway. The solitude is bliss. I can do more work here in a day than I can in a month around people. Cambridge was absolutely unbearable. A brothel. Impossible to concentrate. Here at last I feel I'm solving things.

> WITTGENSTEIN *rows off.*

SC. 12   HAIRCUT

> RUSSELL *is having a haircut.*

HAIRDRESSER   I've heard Herr Wittgenstein has gone to Norway.

RUSSELL   I told him it would be dark.

He said he hated daylight.

I told him it would be lonely.

He said he prostituted his mind talking to intelligent people.

I said he was mad.

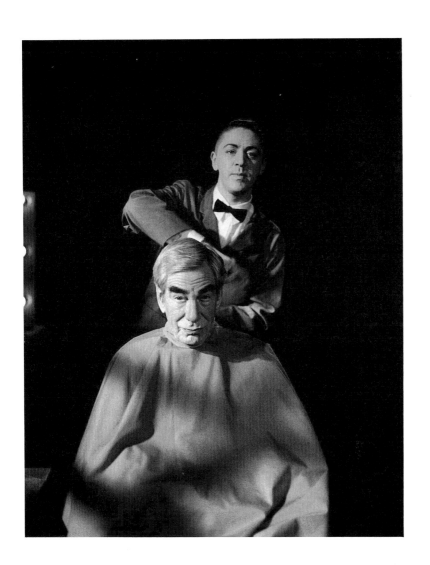

He said god preserve him from sanity.

HAIRDRESSER   God certainly will. It's shocking that he's never read Aristotle.

SC. 13   CERTAINTY

> YOUNG WITTGENSTEIN *and the* MARTIAN *are sitting by the red post box. In the background the signpost reads: TO WORLD WAR 1.*

YOUNG WITTGENSTEIN   I don't merely have the visual impression of a pillar box. I know this is a pillar box.

MARTIAN   I know this is a hand. And what is a hand?

YOUNG WITTGENSTEIN   What?

MARTIAN   This for example, it's a certain certainty.

YOUNG WITTGENSTEIN   I am familiar with certainty.

MARTIAN   I know this film studio is in Waterloo, but how do I know that you are Ludwig Wittgenstein?

> *The* MARTIAN *bites his claw and we hear piano music begin.*

SC. 14   VIENNA 1

> WITTGENSTEIN *turns the sheet music while his brother* PAUL *plays the grand piano.* HERMINE *bursts in – interrupting them.*

HERMINE   Ludwig, Ludwig, I've just heard from Mother that you're going to join up! Now look, I understand wanting to do your bit in this terrible war. But why do you want to die in the trenches? Why not get a clerical job in Vienna?

WITTGENSTEIN   Because I want to go to the front.

HERMINE   Why put yourself at risk like this, Ludwig? You've been exempted for Christ's sake.

WITTGENSTEIN   Standing eye to eye with death will give me the chance to be a decent human being. I'll be doing something.

PAUL   I'm going as well. We've got to do our duty.

> PAUL's *hands crash down on the keys of the piano.*

SC. 15   WW1

> YOUNG WITTGENSTEIN *holds a bright blue flag with gold lettering on it which reads: 'The World is Everything – That is the Case'.*

YOUNG WITTGENSTEIN   Where two principles meet, which cannot be reconciled with one another, then each calls the other a fool or a heretic.

> WITTGENSTEIN *is dressed in a soldier's uniform. He is armed with a machine gun which he fires.*

WITTGENSTEIN   I'm hated because I'm a volunteer. I'm surrounded by people who hate me. The nearness of death will bring me the light of life. God enlighten me. God enlighten me. I am a worm, pray God that I become a man. God be with me. God be with me. Amen.

> *He fires the machine gun repeatedly.*

SC. 16   PRISONER

> *Two prisoners of war play a board game with spent bullets.* WITTGENSTEIN *looks on.*

WITTGENSTEIN   I know this world exists. But its meaning is problematic. Am I good or am I evil? When my conscience upsets my equilibrium, then I am not in agreement with something. What is it? Is it the world? Or is it God?

> WITTGENSTEIN *stands up and cloaks his head in a grey felt blanket.*

SC. 17   POST CARD FROM ITALY

> RUSSELL *and* OTTOLINE *are in bed.* RUSSELL *is reading a postcard sent from* WITTGENSTEIN'*s Italian prison of war camp.* OTTOLINE *smokes and wears an acid green ostrich feather hat.* RUSSELL *is wearing a red dressing gown.*

RUSSELL   Wittgenstein has been taken prisoner.

OTTOLINE   Oh, how fascinating.

RUSSELL   'I am a prisoner of war in Monte Cassino – under the Italians. I hope we shall see each other after the war. Being shot at many times has altered the way I think about philosophy. So has Tolstoy's *Gospel in Brief.* I have written a book called *Tractatus-Logico-Philosophicus.* It combines logical symbolism with religious mysticism. It's better with no shoes – no shoes at all. Love, Ludwig.'

OTTOLINE   I must send him some more cocoa tablets. Sounds like he's rather depressed. Does he know you've been in prison Bertie?

RUSSELL   I doubt it.

OTTOLINE   Such nice manners always, Ludwig. Good stock. What is logical symbolism?

RUSSELL   Too difficult to explain.

OTTOLINE   That's the trouble with you Bertie, you can never answer a straight question.

SC. 18   RELEASED

> YOUNG WITTGENSTEIN *holds a frame of barbed wire. He looks through it and speaks directly to camera.*

YOUNG WITTGENSTEIN   I was released from prison camp on the 21st August 1919. I wanted to get my *Tractatus* published so I went back to Vienna.

Piano music fades in.

SC. 19   VIENNA II

WITTGENSTEIN *still wearing his Hapsburg uniform is turning the sheet music for* PAUL *who plays the grand piano.*

HERMINE   Ludwig! Ludwig, what do you mean you want to teach in a rural school? It would be like a precision instrument opening crates. You were decorated in the war. Bertrand Russell says you're the great philosophical hope. You can't go and teach in the provinces.

WITTGENSTEIN   Hermine, you remind me of someone looking out through a closed window who cannot explain the strange movements of someone outside. You can't tell what sort of storm is raging or that this person might only be managing to stay on his feet with difficulty.

HERMINE   Well, I still think it's a waste of your talents. If you hadn't been so daft and given all your money to us you could publish your book yourself. Without having to bow and scrape to publishers.

WITTGENSTEIN   I don't want to force my philosophy on the world if a publisher won't publish it. Can't you understand that?

HERMINE   Well I would rather have a happy person for a brother than an unhappy saint.

WITTGENSTEIN   I am going to teach.

SC. 20   SCHOOLROOM I

The SCHOOLGIRL *sits at* WITTGENSTEIN*'s desk in the schoolroom. On the blackboard are quotes from* WITTGENSTEIN*'s philosophy. She is having problems reading from her notebook.*

SCHOOLGIRL   Those truth possibilities of its true argument which verify and prositions I shall call its Truth grounds.

WITTGENSTEIN *comes behind her with a cane and bangs on the blackboard. He berates her for not comprehending and pushes her head to the desk.*

WITTGENSTEIN   Yes, good, proposition. So what is this here? What do you call this here? Logic. What's this here? What do you call this here?! Teaching you is a thoroughly unrewarding experience. Do you understand what I'm saying? Do you understand what I'm saying? It's a waste of time. It's a waste of my time, your time, everybody's time. You understand what I'm saying. Do you understand what I'm saying? Oh my god! Oh my dear dear god.

SC. 21   SCHOOLROOM II

YOUNG WITTGENSTEIN *is writing 'loony Ludwig' on the blackboard repeatedly. In the 'oo' of loony he makes cartoon eyes.*

WITTGENSTEIN (VO)   Teaching proved to be a sham. I had to do a runner and lie about my brutality towards the children. They just weren't any good at logic or maths. And they drove me crazy. I kidded myself that my background and class weren't important but I stood out like a sore thumb at these provincial schools. The parents hated me and called me strange. I felt guilty for years. Somehow I had failed – morally.

> YOUNG WITTGENSTEIN *takes off his glasses and cleans them on his shirt.*

SC. 22   RED PILLAR BOX

> YOUNG WITTGENSTEIN *sits on top of the red pillar box talking to the* MARTIAN. *In the background the signpost reads 'TO CAMBRIDGE AGAIN'.*

MARTIAN   This is a red pillar box.

YOUNG WITTGENSTEIN   How do you know?

MARTIAN   I have done my homework. Green is green.

YOUNG WITTGENSTEIN   Children learn by believing adults. Doubt comes after belief.

MARTIAN   I know what I believe. Where I come from there are no adults – and so no doubts.

YOUNG WITTGENSTEIN   If I post this letter to New York, does that strengthen my conviction that the Earth exists?

MARTIAN   The Earth does exist and so do Martians.

SC. 23   VIENNA III

> HERMINE *is arranging a female model on a day bed to paint. A primed pink canvas is on the easel.*

HERMINE   Well you end the book with the line:

'Whereof one cannot speak, thereof one must remain silent.' Why didn't you? I don't understand a word, Ludwig. It's gobble-de-gook. How much were you paid for this?

WITTGENSTEIN   I was paid nothing for the rights and will receive no royalties.

HERMINE   Typical! You won't be able to buy a pair of socks soon.

WITTGENSTEIN   But I have published a book.

HERMINE   I heard that the book was only published because Bertrand Russell wrote an introduction.

WITTGENSTEIN   I have Russell's introduction. He can't understand a word either.

HERMINE   Who can?

WITTGENSTEIN   Hermine, we must improve ourselves. That's all we can do to better the world.

HERMINE   Is it true you're designing Gretyl a brand new house?

WITTGENSTEIN   That's right. The whole thing. Right down to the window latches and the door handles.

HERMINE   Well I hope it's more comprehensible than your book.

SC. 24   GET HIM BACK

> RUSSELL *is on the telephone to* MAYNARD KEYNES. KEYNES *is on his bed being helped to dress by* JOHNNY.

RUSSELL   Maynard, Maynard.

KEYNES   Waistcoat!

RUSSELL   His book is obscure and too short – but good. My introduction got it published.

KEYNES   Yes of course Bertie, but I still think we should get him back to Cambridge.

JOHNNY   Maynard, we're going to be late.

RUSSELL   Well Maynard, you're going to have to sort out his grants. In a moment of amnesia he gave away all his money to his brothers and sisters. An absolute fortune I'm told.

KEYNES   If I can sort out the economies of the world, I ought to be able to sort out a stipend for Wittgenstein. That is if Cambridge will still have him.

RUSSELL   Oh I'm sure they will have him. His *Tractatus* is all the rage – whatever we may think of it.

KEYNES   Leave it to me, I know how to get him back.

RUSSELL   Oh, uh Maynard, hold on a moment. I just ...

They hang up.

KEYNES   Johnny, do you feel like a trip to Vienna?

JOHNNY   Vienna.

SC. 25   MONASTERY

WITTGENSTEIN *is watering a flower bed.* JOHNNY *appears wearing a white track suit.*

JOHNNY   Dr Wittgenstein, Dr Wittgenstein. I've come to take you home.

WITTGENSTEIN   Home. Where's that?

JOHNNY   Cambridge.

WITTGENSTEIN   Cambridge – god help me.

JOHNNY *hands letters to* WITTGENSTEIN.

JOHNNY   I have letters from Mr Keynes and Mr Russell. I should introduce myself – Johnny. Mr Russell asked me to tell you that you're the greatest philosopher of our time.

WITTGENSTEIN *opens the letters.*

WITTGENSTEIN   Oh, tell me Johnny, are you a philosopher?

JOHNNY   Yes.

WITTGENSTEIN   Are you happy? You know, you really should give it up. Get out while you still can.

Piano music fades up.

SC. 26   DANCING IN BLOOMSBURY

KEYNES' *wife* LYDIA LOPOKOVA *is practising her ballet steps.* KEYNES *arrives.*

KEYNES   Lydia!

LYDIA   Ah, Maynard.

KEYNES   God has arrived. He was on the 5.15 p.m. train.

LYDIA   Are you sure it's a good idea bringing him here Maynard? I fear he's difficult and peculiar.

They kiss.

KEYNES   A philosopher is a citizen of no community.

LYDIA   Does he make fit with Bloomsbury friends? He seems so heavy handed and uh, Germanic.

KEYNES   Yes he is.

LYDIA   Why are you all so interesting in him?

KEYNES   Because he's a genius ninoushka.

LYDIA   Yes, but what is he doing?

KEYNES   He's trying to define for us the limits of language and what it is to have communication, one with another.

LYDIA   Don't be so pompous.

KEYNES   Dearest darling, I am going to be pompous. The country needs more than one decent philosopher. Bertie needs some competition. Our Viennese import might just do the trick.

LYDIA   Maynarddoushka – your head is infinitely more flexible than my legs.

> *They burst out laughing and* LYDIA *goes back to her ballet steps.*

SC. 27   DEPRESSION

> WITTGENSTEIN *is fully clothed in bed with his head under the covers.* JOHNNY *comes in wearing a yellow track suit.*

JOHNNY   What are you doing? Everyone's waiting for you.

WITTGENSTEIN   Go away. Please! They're torturing me.

JOHNNY   For god's sake, just open your mouth and say the first thing that comes into your head.

WITTGENSTEIN   Don't be so ridiculous.

JOHNNY   Listen, just get through this seminar and we can go to the cinema.

> WITTGENSTEIN *comes out from beneath the covers and* JOHNNY *strokes his hair.*

SC. 28   SEMINAR I

> KEYNES, RUSSELL *and* SIX STUDENTS *sit in a semi-circle of yellow deckchairs.* WITTGENSTEIN *is at the blackboard drawing a dog.*

WITTGENSTEIN   A dog cannot lie. Neither can he be sincere. A dog may be expecting his master to come. Why can't

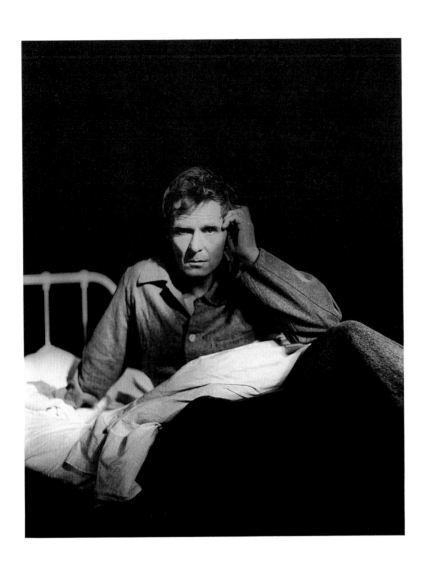

he be expecting him to come next Wednesday? Is it because he doesn't have language? If a lion could speak, we would not be able to understand what he says. Why do I say such a thing?

STUDENT 1   If we can understand him I shouldn't think we'd have too much trouble with a lion.

STUDENT 2   We could get an interpreter.

WITTGENSTEIN   You mean for me or for the lion? Yes, we could get an interpreter. But what possible use would that be? To imagine a language is to imagine a form of life. It's what we do and who we are that gives meaning to our words. I can't understand the lion's language because I don't know what his world is like. How can I know the world a lion inhabits? Do I fail to understand him because I can't peer into his mind?

> WITTGENSTEIN *draws a pineapple on the black-board.*

What's going on behind my words when I say 'This is a very pleasant pineapple'? Take your time.

STUDENT 1   The thought Professor.

WITTGENSTEIN   I see. What is the thought that lies behind the words 'This is a very pleasant pineapple'?

STUDENT 1   This is a very pleasant pineapple?

WITTGENSTEIN   Listen to me. We imagine the meaning of what we say as something queer, mysterious, hidden from view. But nothing is hidden. Everything is open to view. It is just philosophers who muddy the waters.

STUDENT 1   (Slapping his face) Professor Wittgenstein, you can't know this pain. Only I can.

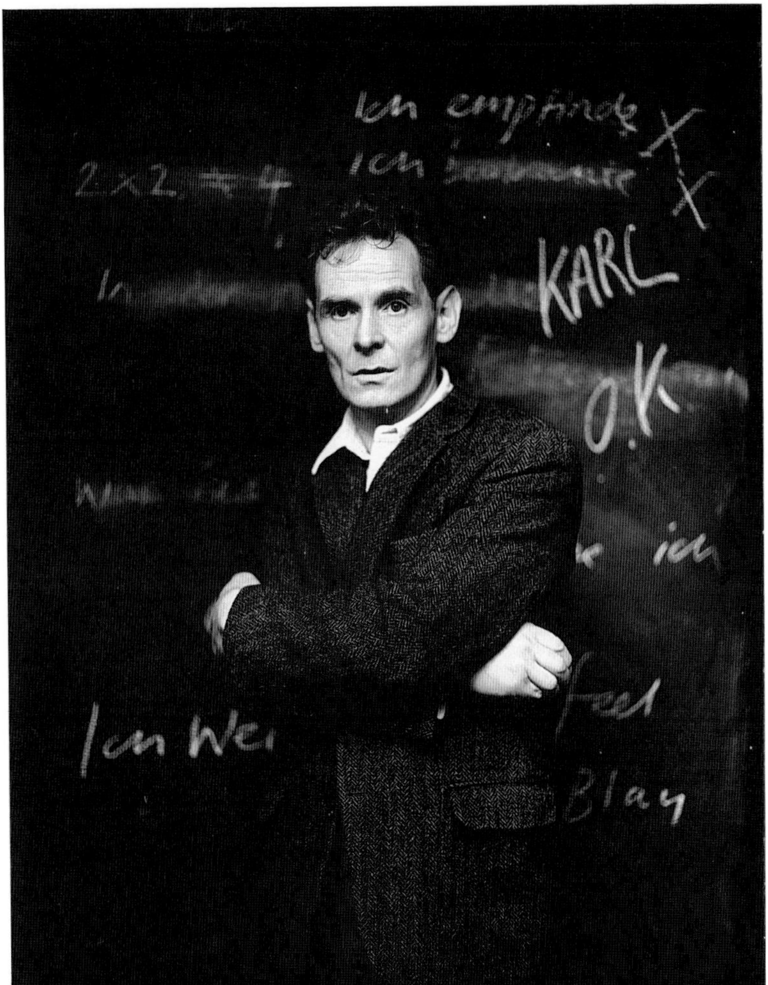
Ich empfinde
Ich
2x2 = 4
KARL
O.K
ich
feel

WITTGENSTEIN   Are you sure you know it? You don't doubt you had a pain just then?

STUDENT 1   How could I?

WITTGENSTEIN   If we can't speak of doubt here, we can't speak of knowledge either.

STUDENT 1   I don't follow.

WITTGENSTEIN   It makes no sense to speak of knowing something in a context where we could not possibly doubt it, therefore to say 'I know I am in pain' is entirely senseless. When you want to know the meaning of a word, don't look inside yourself, look at the uses of the word in our way of life. Look at how we behave.

RUSSELL   Are you saying there are no philosophical problems?

WITTGENSTEIN   There are linguistic, mathematical, ethical, logistic, religious problems – but there are no genuine philosophical problems.

RUSSELL   You're trivialising philosophy.

WITTGENSTEIN   Philosophy is just a by-product of misunderstanding language. Why don't you realise that?

KEYNES   Oh dear, he can't bear disagreement can he?

SC. 29   CINEMA I

> WITTGENSTEIN *and* JOHNNY *are sitting in the front row of a cinema. The projector light beams from behind them. They are fully absorbed in the film.* JOHNNY *wears a yellow tracksuit and is scribbling in a notebook.*

WITTGENSTEIN   What are you doing?

JOHNNY   Making notes on your class before I forget it.

WITTGENSTEIN   Are you mad? You'll ruin the plot.

JOHNNY   Shh. There is no plot.

WITTGENSTEIN   There might be. Put it away. Put it away this instant.

JOHNNY   What did you say about Fortnum and Mason?

WITTGENSTEIN   Don't be ridiculous.

> JOHNNY *puts away his notebook and they look up at the screen.*

SC. 30   CINEMA II

> YOUNG WITTGENSTEIN *wearing 3-D specs, licks a blue ice lolly in the cinema. He does shadow puppets in the light of the projector beam.*

WITTGENSTEIN (VO)   There was no competition between the cinema and seminar. I loved films. Especially Westerns and Musicals. Carmen Miranda and Betty Hutton were my favourite actresses. I always sat in the front row. Film felt like a shower bath, washing away the lecture. I hated the newsreels – far too patriotic. I felt the makers must have been 'master pupils of Goebbels'. As for playing the national anthem at the end – I'd sneak out.

SC. 31   PLANET GAME

> WITTGENSTEIN, KEYNES *and* LYDIA *play the planet game.* LYDIA *as the SUN stands in the centre.* KEYNES *as the EARTH rotates around the SUN. And* WITTGENSTEIN *as the MOON runs around the EARTH. They all hold brightly coloured beach balls to represent the SUN, EARTH and MOON.*

WITTGENSTEIN   Come on Maynard, speed it up!

KEYNES   I can't go any faster, it's making me giddy.

LYDIA   Should I go any faster Ludwig?

WITTGENSTEIN   No, no, you keep going as you are. Come on Maynard, keep it up, keep it up, keep it up. You're slowing the whole thing down.

KEYNES *almost falls over from dizziness.*

KEYNES   I'm done for.

WITTGENSTEIN   You've ruined the whole thing! We were just getting into rhythm.

KEYNES *hits* WITTGENSTEIN *with his ball.*

KEYNES   Go away and play with someone else.

WITTGENSTEIN   All right, you can be the Sun this time. It's easier. I'll be the Earth and Lydia can be the Moon.

LYDIA   We take rest. Take tea. Come along Maynard.

They go off leaving WITTGENSTEIN *perplexed.*

WITTGENSTEIN   Oh dear, I wonder where I went wrong?

SC. 32   THE POEM

RUSSELL *is arranging irises in a vase on his gold desk.* OTTOLINE *wearing a red ostrich feather hat comes in with Julian Bell's satirical poem. She sits on the desk and reads it to him.*

OTTOLINE   Oh Bertie, do listen to this. It's Julian Bell's satirical poem of Ludwig:

'For he talks nonsense, numerous statements makes,
Forever his own vow of silence breaks:
Ethics, aesthetics, talks of day and night,
And calls things good or bad, and wrong or right.
Who, on any issue, ever saw

Ludwig refrain from laying down the law?
In every company he shouts us down,
And stops our sentence stuttering his own;
Unceasing argues, harsh, irate and loud,
Sure that he's right, and of his rightness proud,
Such faults are common, shared by all in part,
But Wittgenstein pontificates on Art.'

SC. 33   BICYCLES

> *Three* WOMEN CYCLISTS *stand behind a bicycle taunting* WITTGENSTEIN.

WOMEN ON BICYCLES   Witters-gitters, witters-gitters, witters-gitters, fairy, fairy, fairy!

WOMAN UNDERGRADUATE   Idiot!

SC. 34   PAINTING A PAINTING

> OTTOLINE *wearing blue is painting a monochrome red portrait of* RUSSELL *at her easel.* WITTGENSTEIN *giving the 'V-sign' asks:*

WITTGENSTEIN   What does this mean?

OTTOLINE   It's a gesture of contempt.

WITTGENSTEIN   A cyclist did this to me as I was crossing the road. I decided then and there to kill myself.

OTTOLINE   Are you coming to the Palladium with us this evening?

WITTGENSTEIN

> *Giving the 'V- sign' again.*

What's the logical structure of this gesture? It doesn't have one! That means I've spent most of my life groping down a blind alley.

RUSSELL   Isn't it rather an overreaction to kill yourself because somebody gives you a V- sign.

WITTGENSTEIN   Philosophy hunts for the essence of meaning. There's no such thing! There's no such thing – just the way we do things in everyday life. Things like that. The college porter knows that.

OTTOLINE   So what are you planning to do for the rest of your life.

WITTGENSTEIN   I shall start by committing suicide.

RUSSELL   Champagne before you go?

WITTGENSTEIN   Uh, I'd ... I'd love a cup of tea.

SC. 35   HOMO EROTIC

> KEYNES *is on his bed reading the* Tractatus. JOHNNY *in yellow pyjamas comes bounding onto the bed.*

KEYNES   How like a philosopher to hate philosophy.

JOHNNY   He thinks ordinary working people have the answers. He wants me to give up philosophy. Perhaps I should. Philosophy just states what everyone admits. How does philosophy take the measure of this?

> *They kiss.*

KEYNES   It's not supposed to. It'd be like complaining that you can't play a tune on a carrot.

JOHNNY   Precisely.

KEYNES   Do you think philosophy is useless?

JOHNNY   Oh no – it serves Ludwig as a therapy.

KEYNES   Are you going to take his advice?

JOHNNY   I was destined for the pits. My parents gave up everything to get me here. I'd be quite happy to go back, but it would break their hearts.

KEYNES *touches* JOHNNY *on the shoulder.*

SC. 36   TEA CHEZ WITTGENSTEIN

WITTGENSTEIN *and* OTTOLINE *are having tea at the grey table. They drink tea from chemistry beakers.*

OTTOLINE   Well, what about Aristotle?

WITTGENSTEIN   What about Aristotle? I've never read Aristotle. What can he tell us anyway? The answers are in Tolstoy, Dostoevsky and St Matthew.

OTTOLINE   Oh how marvellous! I didn't know you were a Christian, Ludwig.

WITTGENSTEIN   I'm not. It's just that I look at everything from a religious point of view. Why is there anything at all, rather than just nothing?

OTTOLINE   Well how the bloody blue blazes should I know? I'm the woman and you're the philosopher.

WITTGENSTEIN   The most important part of my philosophy hasn't been written. I can't write it. It can never be written.

OTTOLINE   Oh bunkum! A full English breakfast and a spot of application.

WITTGENSTEIN   I doubt it will be understood in the future. People, culture, the air. Everything will be different in the future. We're mutating.

OTTOLINE   You know, your obsession with affection is quite, quite ridiculous.

WITTGENSTEIN   I want to be perfect. Don't you?

OTTOLINE   Christ, no!

WITTGENSTEIN   Then I don't see how we can be friends.

OTTOLINE   Neither do I!

SC. 37   SEMINAR II

> WITTGENSTEIN *is giving another seminar.* KEYNES, RUSSELL, JOHNNY *and the* SIX STUDENTS *sit in yellow deckchairs.*

WITTGENSTEIN   I used to believe that language gave us a picture of the world. But it can't give us a picture of how it does that. That would be like trying to see yourself seeing something. How language does that is beyond expression. That is the mystery. That was all wrong. Language isn't a picture at all.

RUSSELL   What is it then?

WITTGENSTEIN   It's a tool; an instrument. There isn't just one picture of the world, there are lots of different language games. Different forms of life, different ways of doing things with words – they don't all hang together.

RUSSELL   What do you mean?

WITTGENSTEIN   All I mean is 'The limits of my language are the limits of my world.' We keep running up against the walls of our cage. I'm terribly sorry – you have a worthless teacher today. I'm all cleaned out. Please forgive me.

> WITTGENSTEIN *in despair, turns his back on his audience and faces the blackboard.* KEYNES *comes over to him and places a hand on his shoulder.*

KEYNES   That was quite masterly.

WITTGENSTEIN   It was frightful.

KEYNES   I don't know, it made me feel like a vegetable.

WITTGENSTEIN   How could it possibly? It doesn't feel like anything to be a vegetable.

> STUDENT 1 *comes up to* WITTGENSTEIN *and* KEYNES.

STUDENT 1   I just can't see it Professor, it somehow just seems natural to me to say 'I know I'm in pain.'

WITTGENSTEIN   Oh, natural. Tell me, why does it seem more natural for people to believe that the Sun goes round the Earth, rather than the other way round?

STUDENT 1   Well obviously because it looks that way.

WITTGENSTEIN   I see. And how would it look if the Earth went round the Sun?

STUDENT 1   Um, well I suppose ... yes I see what you mean.

SC. 38   CINEMA III

> WITTGENSTEIN *and* JOHNNY *are sitting in the front row of the cinema. The projector light beams from behind them.* WITTGENSTEIN *takes* JOHNNY's *hand.* JOHNNY *looks at* WITTGENSTEIN *who stares straight ahead.*

SC. 39   SEMINAR – FLICK

> YOUNG WITTGENSTEIN *sits at* WITTGENSTEIN's *desk. He has feathers in his hair. He is writing in a notebook with a quill.*

YOUNG WITTGENSTEIN   Seminar – flick. Seminar – flick. Flick – seminar. Seminar – flick. Seminar – flick.

WITTGENSTEIN (VO)   On and on it went. Cambridge, Cambridge, Cambridge! No wonder everyone dreamed of

Moscow. Keynes and Russell had both been there. Bertie, always the opportunist, wrote a shilling shocker called *The Practice and Theory of Bolshevism*. He condemned it out of hand but, as everyone knows, the best of the Cambridge lot became spies. My dream was to go to the Soviet Union and work as a manual labourer.

SC. 40   FIXING HIM UP

> JOHNNY *wearing a white tracksuit is doing tai-chi shadow boxing.* WITTGENSTEIN *looks on.*

WITTGENSTEIN   I've fixed you up a job with a local engineering firm.

JOHNNY   Why?

WITTGENSTEIN   I thought you'd be pleased. You'd be working with your hands. You should do something useful.

JOHNNY   But Ludwig, my training's academic. That's the challenge.

WITTGENSTEIN   I'm going to Russia. I shall try to find us both manual jobs there.

JOHNNY   Why do you want to go to Russia?

WITTGENSTEIN   Oh, by the way, you'll have to lend me a tie.

> WITTGENSTEIN *goes off but comes back to kiss* JOHNNY *goodbye.*

SC. 41   SOV U

> WITTGENSTEIN *and* SOPHIA JANOVSKAYA *(Professor of Mathematical Logic at Moscow University) are having a discussion in front of a red flag.*

SOPHIA   Professor Wittgenstein, on behalf of the Institute

of Foreign Relations, I can offer you two things: a chair in philosophy at Kazan University or a teaching post in philosophy at Moscow University.

WITTGENSTEIN   Comrade please, I don't want to teach. I want to work as a manual labourer, either in a factory or on a collective farm.

SOPHIA   (She breaks into Russian ...)

I'm terribly sorry Professor Wittgenstein, but this is absolutely out of the question. The one thing that is not in short supply in the Soviet Union is unskilled labour.

WITTGENSTEIN   Da.

SOPHIA   Da, da, Professor. We must teach the frozen circumstances to sing by playing them their own melody. Professor Wittgenstein, I do recommend you to read more Hegel.

WITTGENSTEIN   (Laughing) I couldn't possibly read Hegel, I'd go stark raving mad. Tell me, have you read Trotsky on Art. That's much more interesting.

SOPHIA   Niet Professor ... (she is shocked and breaks into Russian again) ... Next one.

> She punches a bell on her desk.

SC. 42   THE FACTORY

> JOHNNY *cleaning and polishing a motor bike, sees* WITTGENSTEIN *holding up a red flag with an image of Lenin on it.*

JOHNNY   How was Russia?

WITTGENSTEIN   Well, at least Lenin's state has ensured that there's no unemployment. It is an ordered society. Are you enjoying yourself?

JOHNNY   Yes I am. You were right. Did you find yourself a job in Russia?

WITTGENSTEIN   Sadly no. It looks like I'm stuck with Cambridge and philosophy.

>   JOHNNY *gets up and goes over to* WITTGENSTEIN.

JOHNNY   Ludwig. Give it up.

SC. 43   FALLING OUT

>   WITTGENSTEIN *is planing a piece of wood.*
>   RUSSELL *is very confrontational with him.*

RUSSELL   What the hell are you playing at, Ludwig? I've just been talking to Johnny.

WITTGENSTEIN   What do you mean?

RUSSELL   I mean all this poppycock about engineering and him getting a job. What do you think his parents will think?

WITTGENSTEIN   I haven't the foggiest.

RUSSELL   Johnny's parents are working people. His father's a miner. They sacrificed everything they have to get him to Cambridge.

WITTGENSTEIN   What's Johnny's parents got to do with it.

RUSSELL   Listen Wittgenstein. Johnny's parents are workers. That's what you admire, when it's confined to the pages of Tolstoy.

WITTGENSTEIN   I've never met Johnny's parents.

RUSSELL   I strongly advise you not to. You're foisting your own self-hatred onto their son.

WITTGENSTEIN   You've been reading Sigmund Freud.

RUSSELL   What of it?

WITTGENSTEIN   It's dangerous stuff. Believe me. It takes one Viennese to know another.

RUSSELL   Freud's nothing to do with Johnny sweating it out in some godawful factory. You can't do this Wittgenstein. You can't use Johnny as fodder for your own fantasies.

WITTGENSTEIN   What I do is none of your business.

RUSSELL   It's my business to stop you from – what was your word – 'infecting' too many young men. You have a terrible power over them, can't you see that? Half of Cambridge goes round imitating your mannerisms.

WITTGENSTEIN   You know I've never encouraged disciples.

RUSSELL   I'm talking about you, not your ideas. You lord it over others and you don't even know it. All aristocrats idealise the common folk – as long as they keep stoking the boilers. I should know – I was brought up like that too.

WITTGENSTEIN   If you're talking about my upbringing, that was a long time ago, in another country. How can I possibly speak to a man who believes I corrupt others?

RUSSELL   I'm simply quoting your own words.

WITTGENSTEIN   Russell, I would like you to know that our friendship is now over.

> RUSSELL *goes and* WITTGENSTEIN *continues planing.*

SC. 44   JIGSAW

> KEYNES *is assembling a circular white jigsaw puzzle.* WITTGENSTEIN *looks on disturbed.*

WITTGENSTEIN   I had a fearful row with Russell yesterday. He said I was an evil influence.

KEYNES   What is worrying you Ludwig, is it your logic or your sins?

WITTGENSTEIN   Both. My sins mostly.

KEYNES   Sins, sinners, sinning. What nonsense you do talk. Well you mustn't expect any sympathy from me, I'm not a virtuous man.

WITTGENSTEIN   I never imagined you were. You know, Maynard, every hour, every day, I keep my feet with the greatest difficulty and the slightest gust of dishonesty would be enough to bowl me over forever. That's why people think I'm so strange.

KEYNES   I don't know what to say to you. You're suffering from a terminal case of moral integrity. If you'd just allow yourself to be a little more sinful, you'd stand a chance of salvation.

WITTGENSTEIN   Salvation is the only thing that concerns me. And I know we're not here to have a good time.

KEYNES   Spoken like a true Protestant. Ludwig my dear, there's nothing in the world like the warmth of a sated body.

WITTGENSTEIN   For me it is as if I am being burnt by a freezing wind.

KEYNES   Pull yourself together.

SC. 45   THE CAGE

>WITTGENSTEIN *sits in a suspended cage. In the cage with him is a green parrot in its own cage.*

WITTGENSTEIN   Philosophy is a sickness of the mind. I mustn't infect too many young men. How unique and irre-

placeable Johnny is. And yet how little I realise this when I am with him. That's always been a problem. But living in a world where such a love is illegal and trying to live openly and honestly is a complete contradiction. I have known Johnny three times. And each time I began with a feeling that there was nothing wrong. But after, I felt shame.

SC. 46   SOUL IS A PRISONER

WITTGENSTEIN *and* JOHNNY *are in bed together.*

JOHNNY   What are you thinking?

WITTGENSTEIN   Oh, just some idea.

JOHNNY   What idea?

WITTGENSTEIN   Well, for many years at the centre of philosophy was a picture of the lonely human soul, brooding over its private experiences.

JOHNNY   Yeah, everyone knows that.

WITTGENSTEIN   This soul is a prisoner of his own body, and he is locked out from contact with others by the walls of their bodies. I wanted to get rid of this picture. There is no private meaning. We are what we are only because we share a common language and common forms of life. Do you understand what I'm saying? Do you understand what I'm saying?

> *We flash back to* WITTGENSTEIN *breaking a pencil in frustration at the rural school.*

SC. 47   DOMINOES

> JOHNNY *wearing a blue tracksuit sits beside a gas heater – the blue flames are like a jet engine. He plays dominoes on a silver film case.*

SC. 48   MANNERS

> WITTGENSTEIN *naked in bed is talking to himself*
> *– mocking English upper-class politeness.*

WITTGENSTEIN   Yes ... yes I like that very much. Yes,
Wednesday. Oh ... is that so? Tuesday suits me fine, yes.
Yes, I thought so yes. Yes, he was. Really. Oh Bertie? Yes, I
know him, yes, for many years, yes. Christ.

SC. 49   SEMINAR III

> WITTGENSTEIN *is giving his last lecture.* KEYNES,
> JOHNNY *and* SIX STUDENTS *are sitting in yellow*
> *deckchairs.*

KEYNES   You once said the *Tractatus* had solved all the
problems of philosophy.

WITTGENSTEIN   Yes. So I thought at the time. What I
meant was that I tried to show the sort of things that philosophy could say, and these aren't really important.
What's much more important is all the things it can't articulate.

KEYNES   Doesn't cut the mustard, philosophy. You think.

WITTGENSTEIN   That's right, so I thought at the time. In
fact, I still think so, but for different reasons.

KEYNES   Now talking about your more recent work – the
Philosophical Investigations and so on.

WITTGENSTEIN   That's right. In this later work I abandon
the idea that language is a sort of picture. That's just a mis-
leading metaphor. I mean. You might say that the word
'handbag' is a picture of a handbag. But what about words
like 'hello', 'perhaps', 'oh hell'. What do they give us a
picture of?

STUDENT 2   So how would you now define the relationship between language and the world?

WITTGENSTEIN   Oh, in lots of different ways. My mistake had been to think that there was only one way of talking at stake here. I came to see that there are lots of different things we do with language. Different language games, as I call them. And the meaning of the word is just the way it's used in a particular language game.

KEYNES   And what do you now believe the task of philosophy to be?

WITTGENSTEIN   Philosophical puzzles arise because we tend to mix up one language game with another. For example, people puzzle over the nature of something we call the soul. But this may just be because they're thinking of the soul along the lines of a physical object. They're confusing one way of talking with another.

KEYNES   The job of philosophy is to sort out these language games?

WITTGENSTEIN   Exactly. They're all perfectly in order as they are. Philosophy, in no sense can question them. Philosophy leaves everything exactly as it is.

STUDENT 2   Professor Wittgenstein, you've been associated with the argument that there can't be a 'private' language. Could you explain this a little?

WITTGENSTEIN   What I mean is this. We learn to use words because we belong to a culture. A form of life. A practical way of doing things. In the end we speak as we do, because of what we do. And all this is a properly public affair. Philosophers in the tradition of Descartes start from the lonely self brooding over its private sensations. I want to overturn this century's old model. I want to start from our culture, our shared practical life together, and look at what we think and feel and say it in these public terms.

STUDENT 2   Professor, thank you very much.

SC. 50   A STROLL IN THE RAIN

> WITTGENSTEIN *and* KEYNES *are walking beneath a large green umbrella.* KEYNES *is wearing a violet suit.*

WITTGENSTEIN   I'm thinking of going away.

KEYNES   Not again Ludwig. You've spent your entire life running away.

WITTGENSTEIN   I'm serious, Maynard.

KEYNES   Where to this time? Norway? Vienna? Swansea? Not the Soviet Union again?

WITTGENSTEIN   What's wrong with the Soviet Union?

KEYNES   The place is one enormous labour camp.

WITTGENSTEIN   There's nothing wrong with labour.

KEYNES   There is if they shoot you for not doing it.

WITTGENSTEIN   I want to give up teaching philosophy and concentrate on my book.

KEYNES   Why not do it in Cambridge and be paid?

WITTGENSTEIN   I'm going to Ireland to live by the sea.

KEYNES   In Ireland they shoot you if you work. Oh Ludwig.

WITTGENSTEIN   I know, I'm a complete bloody disaster.

KEYNES   We love you.

SC. 51   IRELAND

> WITTGENSTEIN *sits in a green deckchair.* STUDENT 2 *comes up behind him.*

STUDENT 2   Dr Wittgenstein.

WITTGENSTEIN   Oh, you're here. Good. At last.

STUDENT 2   You couldn't have chosen a more remote place. Well, how's the work on your book?

WITTGENSTEIN   Creeping along.

STUDENT 2   That means you've penned a masterpiece. What's the news from the doctor?

WITTGENSTEIN   Not good I'm afraid.

STUDENT 2   I hope it's not anything serious.

WITTGENSTEIN   Last week I saw a specialist in Dublin. I have cancer of the prostate.

STUDENT 2   Oh, I'm sorry.

WITTGENSTEIN   It responds well to hormone treatment – early stages.

STUDENT 2   Is there anything I can do?

WITTGENSTEIN   Don't think I'm afraid of dying. It is death which gives life its meaning and shape. You can take me back to Cambridge. I don't want to die here.

STUDENT 2   Any time you like.

SC. 52   DEATHBED

> WITTGENSTEIN *is on his deathbed.* KEYNES *sits beside him.*

WITTGENSTEIN   You know, I'd quite like to have composed a philosophical work which consisted entirely of jokes.

KEYNES   Why didn't you?

WITTGENSTEIN   Sadly, I didn't have a sense of humour.

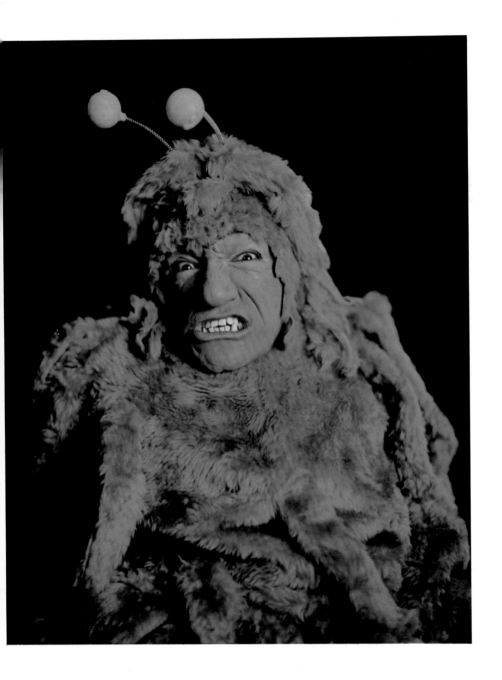

KEYNES' *story is punctuated by images of the* YOUNG WITTGENSTEIN *with a snow man, with a sunset and flying balloons.*

KEYNES   Let me tell you a little story. There was once a young man who dreamed of reducing the world to pure logic. Because he was a very clever young man, he actually managed to do it. And when he'd finished his work, he stood back and admired it. It was beautiful. A world purged of imperfection and indeterminacy. Countless acres of gleaming ice stretching to the horizon. So the clever young man looked around the world he had created, and decided to explore it. He took one step forward and fell flat on his back. You see, he had forgotten about friction. The ice was smooth and level and stainless, but you couldn't walk there. So the clever young man sat down and wept bitter tears. But as he grew into a wise old man, he came to understand that roughness and ambiguity aren't imperfections. They're what make the world turn. He wanted to run and dance. And the words and things scattered upon this ground were all battered and tarnished and ambiguous, and the wise old man saw that that was the way things were. But something in him was still homesick for the ice, where everything was radiant and absolute and relentless. Though he had come to like the idea of the rough ground, he couldn't bring himself to live there. So now he was marooned between earth and ice, at home in neither. And this was the cause of all his grief.

Fade to:

SC. 53   CHROMODYNAMICS

The MARTIAN *sits on* WITTGENSTEIN's *deathbed. He holds a prism which refracts the light.*

MARTIAN   Hail Chromodynamics, Lord of Quantum. This is Quark, Charm and Strangeness reporting. Concerning

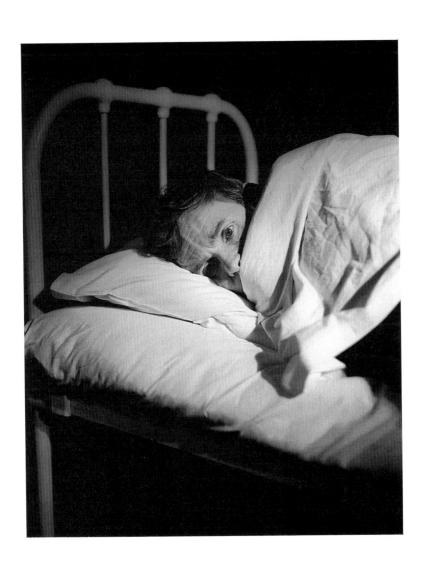

the philosopher Ludwig Wittgenstein. Deceased. The solution to the riddle of life in space and time lies outside space and time. But as you know and I know, there are no riddles. If a question can be put at all, it can also be answered.

Cast in order of appearance:

Young Ludwig Wittgenstein	*Clancy Chassay*
Leopoldine Wittgenstein	*Jill Balcon*
Hermine Wittgenstein	*Sally Dexter*
Gretyl Wittgenstein	*Gina Marsh*
Helene Wittgenstein	*Vania del Borgo*
Hans Wittgenstein	*Ben Scantlebury*
Kurt Wittgenstein	*Howard Sooley*
Rudolf Wittgenstein	*David Radzinowicz*
Paul Wittgenstein	*Jan Latham-Koenig*
Tutors	*Tony Peake*
	Michelle Wade
	Tanya Wade
	Roger Cook
	Anna Campeau
	Mike O'Pray
Martian	*Nabil Shaban*
Ludwig Wittgenstein	*Karl Johnson*
Bertrand Russell	*Michael Gough*
Ottoline Morrell	*Tilda Swinton*
Hairdresser	*Donald McInnes*
Prisoners	*Hussein McGaw*
	Chris Hughes
	Budge Tremlett
Schoolgirl	*Aisling Magill*
Artist's Model	*Perry Kadir*
John Maynard Keynes	*John Quentin*
Johnny	*Kevin Collins*
Lydia Lopokova	*Lynn Seymour*
Students	*Ashley Russell*
	Stuart Bennett
	David Mansell
	Steven Downes
	Peter Fillingham
	Fayez Samara
Cyclists	*Samantha Cones*
	Kate Temple
	Sarah Graham
Sophia Janovskaya	*Layla Alexander Garrett*

Associate Director	*Ken Butler*
Lighting Camera	*James Welland*
Costume Desigr.er	*Sandy Powell*
Music Director	*Jan Latham-Koenig*
Film Editor	*Budge Tremlett*
Art Director	*Annie Lapaz*
Chief Make-up and Hair	*Morag Ross*
Sound Recordist	*George Richards*
Production Management	*Anna Campeau*
	Gina Marsh
Executive in Charge of Production (BFI)	*Eliza Mellor*
Executive Producers	*Ben Gibson (BFI)*
	Takashi Asai (Uplink)
First Assistant Director	*Davina Nicholson*
Second Assistant Director	*Richard Hewitt*
Script Supervisor	*Pearl Morrison*
Focus Puller	*Denzil Armour-Brown*
Clapper Loader	*Debbie Kaplan*
Grip	*Johnny Donne*
Second Camera Assistant	*Araf Khan*
Boom Operator	*Orin Beaton*
Sound Editor	*Toby Calder*
Dubbing Mixer	*Paul Carr*
Music Mixer	*Andre Jacquemin*
Wardrobe Supervisor	*Penny Beard*
Wardrobe Assistant	*Michael Weldon*
Hair and Make-up Assistant	*Miri Ben-Shlomo*
Property Buyer	*Kate Stubbs*
Art Department Standbys	*Melanie Oliver*
	Kevin Rowe
Art Department Assistants	*Karl Lydon*
	Ruth Naylor
	Peter Fillingham
	Mandy Barnes
	Madeleine Morris
Scenic Artist	*Matthew Parsons*
Carpenters	*Jonathan Wells*
	David Williams
Stills Photographer	*Howard Sooley*